Backslider

Michael Premo
with
Ken Walker

Published by
WinePress Publishing
MOUNTLAKE TERRACE, WA 90043

Backslider
Copyright © 1995 Michael Premo
Published by WinePress Publishing
PO Box 440, Mountlake Terrace, WA 98043-0440

All rights reserved. No part of this publication may be reproduced, stored in a retrieval system or transmitted in any way by any means, electronic, mechanical, photocopy, recording or otherwise, without the prior permission of the publisher, except as provided by USA copyright law.

Some names have been changed to protect the innocent and guilty.

Scripture quotations taken from the Holy Bible, New International Version. Copyright 1973, 1978, 1984 International Bible Society. Used by permission of Zondervan Bible Publishers.

Cover photography by Greg Gilbert/Seattle Times

PRINTED IN CANADA

ISBN 1-883893-11-9

Backslider

Table of Contents

PART ONE: CALLED TO PREACH

Introduction...Page 1

Chapter 1: Troubled Youth............................Page 4

Chapter 2: Only The Strong Survive.............Page 14

Chapter 3: Maybe Marriage Will Help..........Page 22

Chapter 4: His Saving Grace.........................Page 26

Chapter 5: Spreading The Word....................Page 36

PART TWO: THE FALL

Chapter 6: Trouble In Atlanta.......................Page 44

Chapter 7: Running......................................Page 55

Chapter 8: Restoration Denied.....................Page 65

Chapter 9: Restoration Achieved..................Page 76

PART THREE: TUMBLING DOWN

Chapter 10: Baiting The Trap.......................Page 88

Chapter 11: Cracked Up...............................Page 93

Chapter 12: Into Treatment.........................Page 103

PART FOUR: CHRISTIANS IN RECOVERY

Chapter 13: The Rocky Road Back................Page 113

Chapter 14: Christian Support.....................Page 117

Chapter 15: Backsliders Everywhere............Page 129

Appendix..Page 141

Dedicated to Sue Premo,
the most virtuous woman
I have ever known!

Introduction

"Michael Premo, it is with much sorrow that we excommunicate you from the Church. We deliver you into the hands of Satan for the destruction of your flesh."

Joseph Woods had once been my pastor, spiritual counselor, a father figure and strong leader who had installed me in a church office at a salary equal to his own. We had traveled across the nation, calling the saints to prayer, planting churches and stirring the body of Christ to action. Now the look on his face bore a mixture of judgment and anger.

As overseer of the small denomination birthed by his church in Alaska, it was Brother Woods' duty to pronounce the judgment and discipline for my backsliding, as determined by the pastors, elders and church officials. Many church leaders had gathered together in Anchorage from around Alaska and the West Coast to witness the "judgment of God."

Someone thrust an official-looking document in my hands. My eyes focused on part of a scripture in bold capital letters: **HANDED OVER TO SATAN TO BE TAUGHT NOT TO BLASPHEME.** Among other things, I was accused of blaspheming God.

My thoughts then wandered aimlessly as various pastors and other ordained officials spent two hours reminding me of my failures. I stood rebuked, reproved, corrected, humiliated and shamed.

Finally, I had to speak up.

"Brother Woods, I am guilty of most of these sins, and many others that only God knows about," I grimaced. "But I don't believe I am guilty of blasphemy. Since the first day of my conversion to Christianity, I have loved and respected God. He is perfect love. In my human weakness and rebellion, I have sinned. But by His amazing grace, He has enabled me to rise from each failure, receive forgiveness and continue to walk in the path He has set before me. Only God knows my heart, and

I don't think that I have blasphemed Him."

Harsh stares greeted my speech.

"You men are going to have a very hard time plucking me out of the hand of God, so that you can cast me into the hands of Satan, No man can pluck me from my Father's hands."

Woods' countenance flushed with anger.

"Your whole life is a blasphemy," he thundered back.

For years I had been one of this man's favorite spiritual sons. He had trained me in the ministry after my initial, unskilled but effective style of preaching the Good News. Primarily because of his influence, I had been ordained as an evangelist at the age of 25; we loved and respected each other. But now our friendship lay in ruins, and the pain stabbed at my heart. Other friends, and brothers from my early days of Kingdom service, refused to acknowledge my existence.

I became an outcast in the very house where I had lifted up the name of Jesus Christ. **Why?** How did such a radical fall from grace come about?

The seeds took root during my youth, and now they were bearing rotten fruit. Like my father, mother and stepmother before me, I was a backslider. As I was to learn: **THE WAY OF A BACKSLIDER IS HARD.**

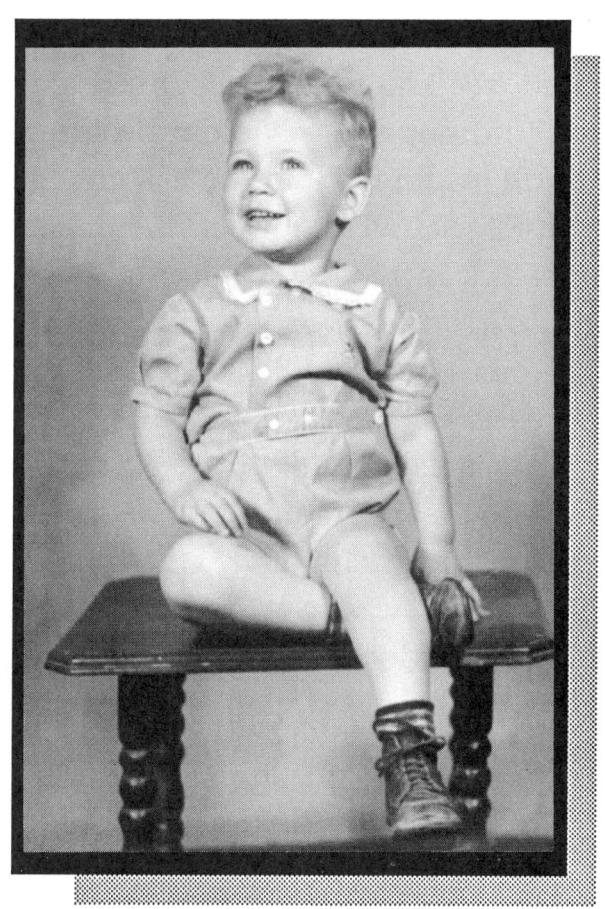

"Dad said I was a good kid"

Troubled Youth

My life began in 1948, in laid back Southern California— before it mushroomed into the Freeway Capital of the world. We lived in one of the West Coast's pioneering subdivisions.

Christmas meant a magnificent brightly-decorated tree and a huge pile of presents beneath it. In the spring, my older brother, little sister and I would flock to the Easter egg hunt in the city park. At Halloween, we dressed up like monsters and lurked in the shadows, pretending to frighten people. Mostly, we were stuffing our over-sized grocery sacks with candy treasures.

Once a year, our family packed up the car and drove to the mountains for a week of camping, fishing, and swimming. Our typical, All-American family was so happy.

I never questioned why my mother had a boyfriend. He always smiled when he gave me rides on his huge Harley Davidson motorcycle.

"Don't tell daddy about my friend," my mom smiled softly one day when I was four. I didn't. A year later, my parents were divorced.

"Mommy and Daddy aren't going to live together any more," they greeted me one morning over breakfast. "Who would you rather live with?"

"I, uh, I..."

I hesitated, trembling as I tried to control shock waves of desperation...

"I...uh...want to live with both of you."

A week later, I spent the night at mom's small apartment. For breakfast, she fixed oatmeal and let me dunk my toast in her hot coffee, smiling at her blue-eyed, blonde, curly-haired little boy. Love filled the room, warming my heart. I loved my mother so much.

When my father arrived to tell me it was time to go, fear gripped me and I screamed hysterically, "No, no!" while clinging to mom's leg. Dad was in good health and over six feet tall, it was easy for him to drag me away.

My heart broke for the first time. As dad rushed me out to the car, I looked back and saw tears flowing down her beautiful face. It would be 14 long years before I would ever see or hear from her again. My sister disappeared with mom; my brother and I stayed with Dad.

Life changed radically. No more Christmas trees, comfortable house, love or security. While a good man, Dad lacked the ability to express affection. The stability of early childhood rode away on a nomadic wave that carried us from Nevada to Michigan and finally deposited us on the beaches of Fort Lauderdale, Florida.

A New Mother

In Florida, our family acquired a newcomer, a stepmother who seemingly stepped from the pages of a novel. Phyllis married dad after a short romance that blossomed in a local bar.

At the time, I was completing my second year of third grade.

We clashed immediately. Before long she and her son moved in with us. My brother and I ran away from home after we overheard her nagging Dad about his "undisciplined" kids.

"Hey, if we're not appreciated around here," My brother Dean whispered to me, "let's move to the mountains and live like Davy Crockett and Daniel Boone."

We sneaked out after dinner. As a mature fifth grader, my brother led the way. We didn't know how far it was to Tennessee, but we set out, pedaling north on Highway A1A. My brother drove while I sat on the handlebars clutching our supplies: peanut butter and jelly sandwiches, a hatchet, and a blanket.

A highway patrolman cut short that escapade, but soon the police shadowed Dean on a regular basis. After the courts ordered him into the state juvenile detention center, Dad moved us to Pensacola.

The year I turned 12 proved to be the finest of my youth: Phyllis and her son vanished a few weeks after we reached Florida's panhandle. Dad and I settled in a little cottage on Pensacola Bay, where I swam and fished. At school, I enjoyed baseball games with my new crop of buddies.

To my dismay, after a year's absence, Phyllis reappeared one afternoon. When I grumbled to Dad, "We don't need her," he responded, "Maybe you don't, but I do."

Though I disliked my stepmother and her alcohol-soaked demeanor, I realized how deeply he loved her. I would adjust.

Phyllis wasn't a bad person, but alcohol destroyed her mind. She often embarrassed and humiliated us. I still remember waiting in the car while dad visited her in the county jail, where she spent time for a burglary that she committed while on a binge.

Several times this self-abuse forced her into mental wards, and as her liquor use intensified, she would share her wild stories with me. One time she claimed to have stolen her son. Supposedly, her own boy died in her arms soon after delivery and she allegedly switched the name tags with a healthy baby and raised the substitute child.

Though I have since made my peace with her, as a boy I especially resented the way she treated my father. One particular incident set my blood to boiling and sunk resentment deep inside my 13-year-old soul.

Dad rarely drank excessively, but that night he returned from a bar with Phyllis, both hopelessly drunk. Two men were with them, and they awakened me around midnight, yelling as they stood in the middle of the road. Phyllis and the strangers wanted to return to the bar, but Dad wanted her to come inside. As she began leaving, he tried to stop her and the men began beating him.

Watching from my bedroom window, I winced at the crunching sounds of their fists on his face as they mercilessly hammered it into a bloody pulp. Finally, my anger exploded and I screamed, "Dad, let the bitch go! She's not worth it!"

He stayed home from work for a week after that, emerging from the bedroom only to use the bathroom or get something to eat. I couldn't stand to look at his scabbed-over, black and blue face. Meanwhile, Phyllis disappeared for about two weeks. Dad and I never talked about that nightmare, or any of the other insane things that intruded into our lives.

I felt guilty, reasoning that I should have protected him. Replaying the fight scene, I would create a new ending, the battle cut short by the threatening sight of me running up with a baseball bat or butcher knife. Shortly afterwards, I joined the Boy's Club and trained to become a Golden Gloves boxer.

Ironically, because of Phyllis's "holy roller"

background I learned about the Pentecostal experience. Phyllis was a backslidden Christian. One day in a startling episode of sobriety, she decided she needed more "religion". God was drawing her back though the god of alcohol fought for her soul to the tragic end.

She insisted we attend a "classical" old fashioned pentecostal church. My brother was released from training school and placed on probation. We sat in the back and eyed a couple cute girls. Soon, Dean and I had straight-laced, Christian girlfriends.

But the church expelled Phyllis because she returned to the bottle. They had dozens of rules — **NO** smoking, drinking, cussing, make-up, bowling, movies, and so on. If anyone did any of those things, they believed that they were hellbound. I often wondered, "Is it possible to meet their religious standards?"

I kept attending that church because of my girlfriend, but usually I ignored the pastor's sermons. It was a shouting church; every so often somebody blasted out with a scream. If a lady fainted and fell to the floor, a deacon rushed to cover her legs with a blanket. Sometimes people would start yelling in tongues.

Despite my inattention, after a short time there I experienced my first contact with God. The preacher was talking about why Jesus died

As he described His pain and agony, I began listening. Love: the reason Jesus shed His precious blood as a sacrifice for the sins of the world. As the power of that love touched my soul, I trembled.

When the pastor concluded, "If anyone wants to get right with God, come down to the altar for prayer," I rose from my pew. Tears filling my eyes, I walked to the front, sank to my knees and prayed. God's love washed over me...so powerful, so righteous, so cleansing. I cried for about 30 minutes.

A week later the church elders asked me to stand in front of the congregation. I nervously obeyed. One of them began speaking with his eyes shut, ending with "Thus saith the Lord".

Later at home I asked Dean what had happened. He grinned, "That man was prophesying that someday you would be a preacher."

However, a couple of weeks later, my girlfriend turned her eyes towards a 16-year-old boy with a fancy car. It may have been puppy love, but my heart was shattered.

"God, I believe in You and You're great," I said after she broke the news, "But I'm too young to be religious. Maybe I'll come back to this when I get old like, maybe 40." I assumed if I died I would go to hell, but I knew I couldn't keep the religious standard that those church people expected.

Highway to Hell

Shortly after leaving the church, I ran away again. We had since moved to Atlanta, Georgia, and I missed my buddies in Pensacola. Clad in madras shorts, T-shirt and tennis shoes, I headed for the highway.

After eight hours of walking and hitchhiking, I climbed into an abandoned car to sleep, and awakened later to the sound of cows grazing in a nearby pasture. The night sounds in the middle of the country 100 miles south of Atlanta drove me back onto the road to continue my journey.

An hour later, I grinned as I saw a car weaving over the road toward me. When the '56 Chevy came to a stop, a voice boomed, "Hey, we're headed for Panama City, boy. Wanna come?"

Jumping in back, I looked up into the face of a black man wearing a huge, silly smile. Two white guys in their late 40s sat up front, and all three smelled like country moonshiners. None of them had any business driving.

"Where you headed, boy?" the driver asked.
"Pensacola."
"You know how to drive?"
"Sure," I lied.
"How old are you?"
"Sixteen," I lied again.

"You have a driver's license?"

Feeling more confident with each lie, I nodded.

"Well, boy, get up here and drive."

I had just turned 14. Thank goodness the car had an automatic transmission and the occupants were so tipsy they would never realize how poorly I handled the steering wheel. Soon we cruised at 50 miles an hour.

Suddenly one of them blurted, "Can't you go any faster?"

"Sure," I smiled, quickly pushing the speedometer up to 70. That brought roars of approval, and before long we zoomed across the terrain at 110 miles an hour.

When we raced into Panama City, the sun lit the sky and I had forgotten about my headlights — although a car whipping across the Panama City bridge at 90 miles an hour didn't need headlights to attract the highway patrol.

"See your driver's license, boy?"

The officer thrust out his hand as the cruiser's red dome light twirled in the morning glare.

"Well," I shrugged, "I don't have one."

"Who's the owner of this car?"

Jerking my thumb behind me, I shrugged, "passed out."

Rousting us out of the Chevy, he marched

us single file to the back seat of his cruiser. Inside the jail, I watched them lock up my companions and asked if I could get a drink.

The fountain stood next to the exit door. I casually leaned over for a sip, then bolted out the back door into the alley. Dashing around the building, I hurdled a fence and scampered towards the bay. Burying myself in some swampy moss for an hour to make sure they had given up the chase, I then casually drifted up the slow-moving current until I spotted a road that led away from town toward Pensacola.

When I finally arrived at a friend's home, my buddies were glad to see me, but my radical behavior alarmed them. Most wore the clean-cut, athletic look. Nonetheless, their eyes couldn't mask their envy when we sat around and I monopolized center stage, puffing on cigarettes while alternately blowing smoke rings and acting cool.

But my days on the road proved to be short lived. After several burglaries, the police had my number. A couple of times they confronted me but I outran them. They finally cornered me hiding under an old southern house. "Come out you rabbit!" they commanded as they shined a flash light into my face. No matter where my wild impulses carried me, in the twinkling of an eye I inevitably found myself back in Atlanta at the juvenile detention center.

I didn't like it there, nor did I care for the punishment when I broke the rules: a steady diet of peanut butter sandwiches without jelly. Yet the pain of that institution was no worse than having to go to another new school, where I had to "fit in" and make new friends.

I hated my unstable life — but outwardly I professed to love moving around, seeing new sights and living new adventures. So when my stepmother and I tore into each other one evening at our newest trailer home by the airport, I resorted to the easiest solution.

"Maybe it would be a good idea to run away again," I raised my eyebrows.

"Want me to pack your bags?" Phyllis deadpanned.

With $6.00 in my pocket I hitchhiked to Florida, eventually getting busted in New Orleans. Back to the Atlanta Juvenile detention center I went for more of the "same O, same O."

2

ONLY THE STRONG SURVIVE

Over the next two years, when I wasn't running away from home, I studied hard — in Crime School. By age 16 I had achieved the status of skilled burglar. Deciding to again seek greener pastures, Dad and Phyllis moved to Pennsylvania, while I chose to stay behind and make it in Atlanta the best way I could.

Suddenly forced into another survival mode, I quickly learned that male prostitution represented easy money. Selling my body in downtown Atlanta, I located one client who bought me clothes and gave me a shiny 1956 Chevy convertible. If the opportunity presented itself, my hustler friends and I robbed our "johns," resorting to violence if necessary.

I didn't particularly care for this method of earning quick cash, but we had to feed our high-flying lifestyle. The "InCrowd" approved — even our girlfriends. When we weren't guzzling beer or whiskey, we set off on joyrides to Florida, breaking into homes along the route to grab whatever we found of value. Several diamond rings decorated my key chain, but with each heist I moved closer to the Law.

Once when we broke into a ritzy home on Pensacola Beach, I decided to take a shower. As I toweled off, my partner screamed, "The cops are here!"

Jumping into my Levi's, I scampered down the beach, but Allen wasn't as fast. He spent a year in jail, while I hitch-hiked back to Atlanta, barefoot and shirtless.

"That's it," I thought. No more school, no more rules. I'll get serious and commit more burglaries, save up lots of cash and get married.

I described the plan to my girlfriend Beverly as we drank beer at Lake Spivey one boiling summer afternoon.

"Me and a couple friends are hoppin' a jet and flyin' to Miami," I said. "When we get back, I'll have $100,000 and you and I can get married and live happily ever after."

"No," She shook her head as my eyes opened wide. "What's gonna happen is you're gonna get busted, thrown into prison, and I ain't gonna see you anymore. Please don't go."

"Nah," I insisted. "That ain't gonna happen.

We know what we're doing, Bev, we've done all this before. I'll be back. You'll see. Start thinkin' what kind of wedding dress you'd like to wear."

Within a week, her prophecy came to pass in the headlines of the ***Fort Lauderdale News:*** "Three High Living Youths Captured."

We had pulled off one too many daytime escapades, and then foolishly checked into the Yankee Clipper Hotel to enjoy the fruits of our labors. Our dreams of easy living lasted as long as the cigarettes we were smoking.

Suddenly the police barged into our room and led us away in a string of handcuffs.

The authorities in Atlanta had already been looking for me, so the cops in Florida were happy to cut a deal: "You take care of him up there and we can forget about him down here."

I landed in a Georgia State Penitentiary surrounded by an electric fence.

The Prison Jungle

Prison is a jungle where the animals are human. Only the strong survive, but nobody escapes unscarred. The sounds of the jungle fill the air with screams of violence, perversion, fear, hatred, loneliness, pride, and broken hearts. Homosexuality is the sick norm, and it rears its ugly head with the demand: fight or be raped. If you're unlucky, you can fight and still be raped.

The guards knew what was going on, but didn't care. Paid $1.75 an hour plus room and board, these kings of the jungle carried clubs to enforce their rule. Some were as inhuman as hardened convicts. One night I overheard a guard offer a reward of one dime for "jacking up" an inmate he didn't like. A muscular assassin eagerly walked over to the skinny, shaking victim and quickly blasted him with a left hook that knocked him senseless. With a smile, the abusive con walked back and held out his hand.

Back in the mid-1960s, the old ways reigned in the South. Never was I so thankful for my earlier Golden Gloves training. I fought and survived, but it wasn't easy.

The guards clubbed inmates for talking in the chow line, since that was against the rules. In fact, they salivated every time they caught someone disobeying the rules. If you fought back, you spent 30 days in the "hole," a small, bare, cement-floor cell. Amenities included an old blanket, coffee can restroom, and a menu of bread and water. A feast of beans and cornbread arrived every third day.

Other than a G.E.D. diploma, I received little useful education there. In fact, most of what I learned had nothing to do with school. I learned how to "beat the system" by learning about my rights and keeping my mouth shut

— especially when guilty. In addition, the time in prison hardened my heart, as did my lack of contact with the outside world. During my three years of confinement, I received a total of three letters and four visits. Beverly, of course, found a new boyfriend.

There was no Christian movement in the prisons then. I saw thousands of inmates come and go and never saw one stand up to be counted as a disciple of Jesus. While the prison chaplain was a pleasant man, he was quite liberal and never preached the gospel. We attended chapel services only when we could lustfully stare at the women in a visiting choir.

About a month before my release, my mother wrote to me for the first time in 14 years, inviting me to return to Southern California to live with her. She had remarried and her second husband wanted to help me. "Wow!" I thought. "A miracle! That sure beats a new suit, eight bucks and a bus ticket back to Atlanta."

Family Reunion

When I walked out of the prison gates in 1968, a time warp greeted one surprised ex-con. Psychedelic clothes, free love, and LSD had become quite fashionable. Now I wouldn't have to sniff glue or typewriter cleaner to get high, nor resort to home brews like aftershave lotion flavored with Kool-Aid. A new life awaited me at the other end of a jet ride to Los Angeles, land of the Hollywood stars. Excitement pulsed through my veins.

My mother met me in L.A., greeting me with a bear hug and her ever-witty personality, which quickly put me at ease. I knew I had to learn some discipline, especially how to control my filthy prison vocabulary. Mom helped me glide back into reality. Making up for lost time, she bought me a 1958 Corvette, hard-top convertible, with black leather interior. I cruised through Beverly Hills, fantasizing that some sexy, rich movie star would "discover" me and take me home with her.

The second week out, mom took me to a fancy nightclub to celebrate. We talked, danced and drank till we were drunk. When we finally stumbled home, I headed straight for my bedroom. Mother followed me in to give me a goodnight kiss. She didn't stop there. Soon she was sensually kissing and rubbing me, and though uncomfortable, my drunken flesh didn't resist.

The next day, I had to deal with the shame and guilt of incest. The voice of demons began to whisper in my ear, reminding me of my earlier perversions. I had to fight to maintain my sanity.

The incest had increased the confusion I combatted as I tried to decide what to do with my life now that I was a "free" man again. I tried to join the Army, but my prison record drew an automatic rejection. Not knowing much else, I chose the familiar habit of burglary. In practically no time, life had become quite complicated, and I wondered, "What is the purpose? Is anybody 'normal'?"

Given the free-flowing drugs in California, it was easy taking up with LSD and on down the line until I arrived at heroin. The first time I stuck a needle in my veins and felt the "rush" flooding my body, sweat poured off my face and I felt myself losing control. But when I realized I wouldn't die, I reasoned that all drugs were acceptable.

In my drug-fogged state, nobody could have convinced me abuse represented a one-way ticket to destruction. Thus, Dad's letter didn't even phase me. He wrote to tell me that — at the age of 41 — Phyllis was dead. She was burned alive along with burning my Dad's house down. Though I ignored it, the message clearly warned: **THE WAY OF A BACKSLIDER IS HARD.**

My mom was a backslidden Christian, she became a runner, dashing down life's fast lane. If it felt good, she did it. Yet she lived with a lot of mental and spiritual pain, searching for comfort and relief through alcohol and wild living, only to discover more pain. Her alcohol and cigarette abuse was beginning to break her body down.

An attractive woman, her personality made her even more beautiful. She was a hard worker, kind and generous, and people enjoyed her company.

Before she died, several years later she quit running, settled down and restored her relationship with God. When I went to visit her during the last days of a losing battle with cancer, she had peace in her soul and a glow on her face. We talked about the things of God and we prayed together. I hugged her and told her I loved her. I look forward to our reunion in heaven where there will be no more pain and all tears will be wiped away.

3

MAYBE MARRIAGE WILL HELP

I met Rose on a blind date. We dropped Acid together one night and a week later we were engaged. Six weeks later, we were married at a backyard ceremony at Mom's house. Following a drunken reception, we drove my Vette to Las Vegas for our honeymoon. Three hours after our arrival, I had blown all our cash at the gaming tables; three months later we separated.

Rose moved in with her old boyfriend, then came back, establishing the on-again, off-again pattern of our marriage.

I was serving some time for a burglary in the Orange County work farm when it came over the intercom that I was the proud Daddy of a healthy baby boy. We made a serious vow to stick together when Michael, Jr., came into our life. Our beautiful baby boy had blue eyes and curly hair.

Though we loved each other, our immaturity constantly ruined the best of intentions. We fought a lot, and Rose often became violent: during our flare-ups, I was the one locking myself in the bathroom. Once she threw a butcher knife at me in the kitchen, and after ducking, I looked up to see the blade quivering where it had jammed into the wall.

I had taken up house painting to make a living. But I couldn't keep a job, since it interfered with my free and easy lifestyle. I loved to gamble, spending up to 30 hours a week in the company of cards. Despite the ulcer I was developing at 20, I refused to quit drinking. In no time, our vows to stay together dissolved once again.

While we were apart, I picked up a barefoot hippie in Costa Mesa as he walked down Sunflower Street. He startled me first by flipping through his Bible and talking about Jesus, then again when he invited me to Bible study at a small church called Calvary Chapel. I had passed the church many times, but because of its architecture and the overflowing parking lot, I had assumed it was a Mexican restaurant.

The following week, I sat in a Sunday night service, amazed at all the longhairs mingling with straight-looking types, young and old. The flowing hair and bushy beard of one preacher, Brother Frisbee, contrasted wildly with the bald-headed senior pastor, Chuck Smith.

I felt the warmth of love and peace there. None of this resembled the strict surroundings that I remembered from that little pentecostal church in Georgia. Excitement surged through my body, but as I thought of returning to God, I sighed, "No, I'm still too young for this religion thing."

Meanwhile, my habits were about to land me in the "big house" for a second time, since California's tolerance of my burglary habit was rapidly approaching Georgia's level. I decided the best route for me lay up the Alaskan highway. On three years' probation for my last break-in, I knew the cops wanted to nail me for another.

"The cops are after me for burglary," I told Rose when I stopped at the beauty shop where she worked as a hairdresser. "I'll probably never see you again."

Seeing the desperation in my eyes, she grabbed hold of my arms.

"I want to go with you."

Packing our meager possessions in our Toyota, along with $350 and a bag of marijuana, we drove north. At the Canadian border, we hid our dope in little Michael's diaper and drove on to Anchorage, finally settling in Indian, a little town 30 miles to the south.

Surrounded by water and mountains, I enjoyed the scenery by walking through the woods on LSD, imagining I was a big game hunter as I shot rabbits and squirrels. For a few months, I worked in the oil fields on the North Slope, but the 70-hour weeks quickly soured and we returned to Anchorage. Rose went to work at the beauty shop and I stayed home to to baby sit.

While smoking pot one afternoon, I decided our apartment needed some decorations. Since we couldn't afford any, I drove to the local department store for a shoplifting tour. I loaded up a shopping cart and calmly wheeled it out to the car. As I loaded my booty into the trunk, an off-duty security guard stuck an iron grip on my arm.

Hiring a good lawyer, I pleaded innocent. Any good criminal does that, even when caught red-handed. After all, a smart attorney can help people avoid paying for their crimes. Not surprisingly, they postponed my case.

Now I faced a four-month wait before my next court appearance and soon my paranoia had surpassed the level that inspired me to leave California. Clinging to our apartment, I would get loaded and daydream about the cops who were waiting outside, trying to pin something big on me so they could put me away for good.

Someone was waiting, all right. But it wasn't the law.

4

HIS SAVING GRACE

"What do you think about God?"

"What?" I thought in amazement. "This is pretty freaky. Here we are, tripping on LSD, listening to Led Zeppelin and Neil Young, and this bisexual hairdresser is asking me about God?"

We had invited Rose's co-worker over for a night of partying. God works in mysterious ways and at times when we least expect Him. So when this dude whipped out a little Bible and started asking me questions I was surprised, but I wanted to talk.

"I believe God is perfect love," I answered, "and one of these days I'm going to take my kids to Sunday School."

"Why don't you turn on to God right now?" he challenged. "Because it ain't like taking a drug when somebody turns on to God," I solemnly replied. "God's trip is eternal, not just for a day or a couple hours. To follow Jesus is radical. I'm not sure I want to pay the price."

Without warning, a Presence settled over me. Through my earlier church experience, I quickly recognized the Holy Spirit. I needed to choose life's course. Who would I serve?

"Hey, man," I broke the hush after my sermonette, "I've got some serious thinking to do. I have to go lie down."

Rose joined me in the bedroom after he left. Lying in the dark, I pondered the changes that would be required in my life.

"Michael, I love you more than your mother, father, wife, children, or best friends," the still, small voice said. "I will give you the love and security you've been searching for."

Those words were so alive and so soothing that my spirit began jumping up and down, screaming "Yes, yes, yes!"

But my carnal mind argued, "NO WAY, MAN! You can't do that! You don't even wanna do that!"

As the war raged, my flesh pressed its case.

"If you go for God, you'll have to go to church again, read the Bible, do all those religious things. You'll have to quit drugs, alcohol, stealing, partying. What about all that other stuff? You ready to go punch in 40 hours a week?

"Yeah," I thought, "that is tough. Is God worth it?"

The turmoil continued, but finally I decided

the insanity and emptiness had reached its peak. Turning to Rose, I spoke as a matter of fact, "For the rest of my life, I'm serving God. And so are you." "Okay," she replied. Of course I really didn't know what I was doing and had no business forcing my wife to take such a serious leap of faith. I just knew it would be easier if we did it together.

After a period of silence, she asked, "Now that we've turned on to God, aren't we supposed to feel something?"

"Be cool. Everything will happen in its right time."

But I wondered: are we supposed to feel something? And what are we to do next? I didn't know any scriptures, and we didn't even have a Bible.

Saved by grace

When morning came, I checked the phone book and dialed the number of a Southern Baptist pastor named Virgil Chron.

"Preacher, you don't know me...I haven't been a faithful churchgoer." I paused, knowing what had to be said. "Last night I took LSD," I confessed, "but I need some spiritual guidance. Could you come over — and bring your wife? Mine is shy, so maybe another woman would help put her at ease."

The attractive, middle-aged couple quickly made us feel comfortable after they sat down in our living room. Virgil asked if we believed that Jesus died on the cross so our sins could be forgiven, that He was raised from the dead after three days, and is still alive, seated at God's right hand.

To each question, we enthusiastically answered, "Yes!"

"All we have to do," Virgil smiled, "is pray and have a little talk with God and this issue will be settled forever."

Joining hands, we knelt on the living room floor. The pastor prayed and then asked us to join in: "It doesn't have to be long or fancy. Just say what's on your heart."

Rose had no religious background, so she started praying to the preacher. He interrupted, "Honey, if you pray to me, I can't do anything. Only God can answer prayer and forgive sin."

Tears came pouring out when Rose resumed. "Please, God, forgive me of my sins and help me to be a good wife and mother!" she sobbed.

"God, I want to follow you for the rest of my life," I followed. "I've done a lot of rotten things, but could you please forgive me?"

I didn't get emotional, but I knew He had heard.

"Praise the Lord!" the pastor said when we

finished. "You two just had your names written in the Lambs Book Of Life. You are born again and are going to spend eternity in heaven."

We accepted their invitation for church, and when they left, I dashed to the bedroom, grabbed my marijuana and dumped it in the toilet. As the pot swirled down the commode, I returned to the living room and flung my cigarettes into the trash.

"That preacher didn't say we had to quit smoking," Rose gasped.

"I know. I just felt it would be the right thing to do."

At 22, neither of us had any nice church clothes, so Sunday morning we donned jeans and clean shirts and nervously set out for church, fearful of how we would be received.

As we nestled into a pew, I noticed my Afro-style hairdo and beard marked me as the congregation's sole hippie. But the choir sang beautifully and the song leader spoke in a Texas accent as he plucked his guitar. Virgil saw us and waved, and we smiled in appreciation. I relaxed.

At the end of his sermon, we quickly responded to the invitation for new members. People clapped and praised God when Virgil shared what had happened that week. Many of them greeted us with huge hugs and smiles, humbling us.

That week I secured a job painting at a military base, a tough job calling for 10-hour days, 6 days a week. But working no longer bothered this new creation. As I worked, I thought about God and told my co-workers about Him and our "cool" church. Every Wednesday night I headed straight from work, paint speckled throughout my fuzzy hair.

Troubling Temptations

The first test of my faith occurred on the job when a curse word inadvertently slipped out of my mouth. I immediately sensed the Holy Spirit's conviction and asked forgiveness, and cursing never again posed a problem. It was a trifle compared with the trial that would soon be dumped in my lap.

Jill, Rose's 16-year-old sister, flew up from California for the summer. Within a week, she accepted Jesus as I read a gospel tract, explaining how a person receives salvation. Before I finished, she dissolved into tears and offered a prayer of repentance.

However, salvation is no guarantee against temptation. The devil loves to pursue new Christians in an attempt to drag them back into the muck of sin. In our case, he eagerly sought to kill two birds with one affair.

Jill initiated the flirting through her filmy nightgown. It displayed her nicely-proportioned features each morning as her seductive eyes beckoned to me. Though part of me wanted to be good, another part of me still wanted to be bad. Despite my fear of getting caught, and my aching desire to be a good husband, I fell into the trap.

Our liaison lasted a week, and afterward I felt so ashamed. I had to swallow all of my pride as I asked God for forgiveness. How hard to admit our mistakes (sins) and turn from our bloated self-image! Yet when I did, I felt our relationship had been restored.

Not so for Jill, who took to dating several men. I asked forgiveness for being a poor example, but her stone-cold look said the damage had been done. When I tried reasoning about "getting right" with God, she rebuffed me.

"If you don't stay out of my business, I'll tell my sister about our affair."

"If you do, I'll have to face whatever I deserve."

I spotted trouble a few days later when a yellow cab drove up to my job site and Rose jumped out. The fire in her eyes appeared far more menacing than the butcher knife in her hand.

"How could you rape my little sister?" she screamed.

"I deserve whatever punishment you want to dish out, but I didn't rape her!"

Broken and humbled, I pleaded, "I was wrong. I'm sorry. Will you forgive me?"

"No, no, no!"

"Look, let's go back and talk to her. I don't know why she made this up, but I did not force myself on her."

When she calmed down, we returned to the apartment, where Jill stubbornly clung to her story. Rose finally chose to believe me and shipped her sister back to California.

Fishing For Men

That setback could have easily claimed our Christianity, but we kept attending church, which helped sustain us. The messages speeded the healing process:

* God forgives when we admit our sin and ask for forgiveness.
* Resist the devil's guilt and condemnation.
* Jesus' cleansing blood makes us white as snow
* God's love is a miracle.

My commitment to the Lord grew. Because of the church's emphasis on evangelism, I became a "soul winner." I carried my Bible everywhere and shared Jesus with anyone, including hitchhikers we intentionally picked up to evangelize:

"Are you high?" I greeted the red-haired, scraggly bearded hippie.

"No way, man," he nervously shook his head.

"We are!"

"You are?"

His face danced.

"What you got?"

"Jesus."

"Wow, I ain't never had none of that."

Leading him to the Lord whetted my appetite, but my true test of boldness arrived with my court date for shoplifting. Before the hearing, I felt God telling me to fire my lawyer because Jesus would be my advocate. When I told my attorney, he looked at me like I had just arrived from outer space. I prepared for the jury trial by asking church members to come and support me in prayer. I wanted God's will done.

After the officer told the jury, "I caught him with the stolen goods and he deserves to go to jail," it was my turn. Bible in hand, I called Pastor Chron as my first witness.

"I believe the rebellious wild lifestyle is all behind Michael," he said. "He is clearly a changed person."

"I pled temporary insanity to this charge because I was temporarily crazy, but since that incident of thievery I have become a new person," I then testified. "The Bible says, 'if any man be in Christ he is a new creature, the old things are passed away and all things become new. Your honor, shortly after I stole that stuff I converted to Christianity. I confessed my sinful life to God and He has forgiven me. I am no longer the same person. God has performed surgery on my heart."

"The man who stole that stuff was nuts, so crazy he left his children alone at home. But God has healed my mind. I'm new. I don't do drugs anymore. I quit drinking and I even quit smoking cigarettes. I quit cussing and the biggest miracle is that I started a steady job. I rest my case and pray the Lord's will be done."

The judge smiled, but the faces in the jury box broadcast a mixture of skepticism and wonder. They quickly found me guilty, but the judge was still smiling when he asked me to stand.

"Young man, I'm going to fine you $300..."

I gulped.

"...But I'm going to suspend that and sentence you to 30 days in jail."

"Thirty days will be easy compared to three years," I thought.

"But I'm going to suspend 27 of them. I'm going to deduct a day for the time you served after you were caught and I'm going to knock off another day if you're good the day you're in there."

Behind me, church members were praising the Lord and chuckling with joy.

"Michael, when would you like to spend your day in jail?"

"Well, I'm busy tomorrow. How about Thursday?"

5

BECOMING A PREACHER

"I want you to be a preacher for Me."

That soft-spoken voice. The same one I heard the night of my acid trip. As we drove to Sunday School, I turned to Rose and said, "God just spoke to me."

"What did He say?" she smiled warmly.

"Ain't tellin'."

I should have been overjoyed to hear from Him. Like Moses, I trembled with fear.

"How can I be a preacher?" I fretted. I was educated on the street and in prison, and I speak terribly.

But the Holy Spirit quietly ministered to me, reassuring me that if I were willing, God would supply the resources. A smile crept across my face as I realized, "God will be my teacher!"

Suddenly a revelation struck: I was ordained by God to be a minister. God had laid His hands on me, anointing me to spread His Gospel. Like a forest flames kindled by a blast of wind, a fire now burned within my soul. After Sunday

School I told our pastor what had happened, he beamed, "I'm with you all the way." After his sermon he announced to the congregation that Mike Premo was surrendering his life to the call of the ministry. After the service many lined up to encourage me with words of faith and support.

A week later, the local prison invited me to deliver the Sunday sermon. Using John 3:16 as my text, I spoke simply and from the heart.

"You have sinned against God," I told the inmates. "All have sinned against God and fallen short of His glory. If you do not have your name written in the Lamb's Book of Life, you will be cast into the Lake of Fire. It isn't God's will that you be lost, but your sin has separated you from Him.

But there is hope! God loves you in spite of your rebellion and lawlessness. He so loves you that He gave His only begotten Son to die on a cross and shed His innocent blood for you. If you believe this, then you can have your sins forgiven and have eternal life. Will you accept God's love or will you reject His love?"

I continued to preach at the prison weekly as the Lord also began to open doors for me to minister at other places.

After our congregation licensed me as t Southern Baptist minister, some young music ministers and I formed an evangelistic outreach called "J.C. & Company."

Some people called me a Jesus Freak

I first entered the pulpit wearing overalls and shaggy hair. Though I later bought a double-breasted, gold velvet suit and a purple tie, I usually stuck with informal attire so I could relate to the young people caught up in the same type of sin that had lured me into so much trouble.

Our first invitation came from the First Baptist Church of Anchorage, and the night we came its midweek crowd swelled from the usual 50 to 800. Five area pastors attended to check us out.

After the band played four praise-filled Christian rock tunes, I strode out in my overalls, a paisley shirt and Brogan boots. So full of the Holy Spirit I felt like I was floating, I began speaking by a supernatural boldness and love. Preaching Christ and Him crucified, I told the overflow crowd that Jesus loved them more than their parents, spouses, children, or best friends. At the end, people flocked to the altar, so many not a space stood empty. As people knelt and wept, we watched in awe.

The nine of us continued to minister across the state, the band thumping out its gospel rock and God anointing my unpolished preaching. The Southern Baptist State Evangelism Conference asked me to be their main speaker on their final evening of the yearly gathering. The band played and then I preached. Only a Christian for 10 months, I addressed a crowd of over 1,000 and saw more than 50 people respond to the altar call for salvation.

In our weakness God was using us to proclaim His message of love. That year we witnessed approximately 2,000 souls converted to

Christianity through our evangelistic meetings. It was a great time of learning and experiencing God's presence and grace.

Trouble At Home

In spite of God's evangelistic wonders, two other matters demanded my attention — my marriage and the California criminal charges that had spurred my exodus to Alaska.

Because I had been traveling so much, my wife and children were starving for affection, attention, and leadership. Naive and ignorant, I dove into the waters of Godly service, assuming Rose would understand. I failed to understand that she was not trained for spiritual battle. In reality we were both babes in Christ. I was able to grow and be strong in God because of my continual fellowship with strong Christians. But Rose was home babysitting and taking care of the house. I failed to effectively minister to her spiritual needs. Because of my neglect I began to see my home fall apart.

As our relationship strained at the seams, she rebelled, smoking cigarettes to upset me or making mean faces while I was in the pulpit. I tried to cope by ignoring her fits or quoting scripture to her. Neither helped restore my out-of-balance home to its proper order, and my lack of time for my wife reaped a sorrowful harvest.

One day as I was studying in my office, Rose walked up and casually announced, "Oh, I had sex with one of your best friends." Heart sinking, I silently asked the Lord for help. He gave me the courage to say, "I understand and I want you to know that I forgive you. I still love you very much. This is a bad experience, but it's history and I won't bring it up again."

A week later, she confessed that she had "blown it" again. She went to a pastor's wife for counseling. She told the truth about her affairs, but complained I was a "fanatic."

"Maybe he's like the apostle Paul," the counselor said. "It might be better if you divorced Michael and married his friend."

With counseling like that, it's no wonder divorce wracks the Christian community as badly as the rest of the world. The cycle of Rose's affairs continued until J.C. & Company finally disbanded and we left for California. I felt it was time for me to turn myself in to the law for my previous crimes. I was prepared to go back to prison for my probation violation and also for a separate burglary that I committed before coming to Alaska.

In Orange County, I divided my time between reporting to the probation officer, preaching, and spending time with my family, including our newest member Joshua. God blessed us with another healthy beautiful baby boy.

When my court date arrived, I went before the judge backed by more than 100 letters of recommendation from pastors and believers across Alaska. I delivered my testimony in court again, trusting that God's will would be done. Because of my long record and the seriousness of my crime Rose and I expected that I would be behind bars before the day was over.

When I finished, the judge peered over his glasses. "Mr Premo, it is obvious you are rehabilitated. I see no value in sending you back to prison. You are sentenced to three years' probation and no jail time. You're free to go back to Alaska and resume your ministry."

Success and Honor

Joseph Woods, founding pastor of the Anchorage Community Church, invited me to join the staff as an evangelist. Just three years after starting my walk with the Lord, I secured a position of great honor. The congregation's attendance had doubled two consecutive years, forming the largest interdenominational church in the state.

As church evangelist, my job description was to inspire and teach the people what the Bible says concerning evangelizing. I taught in Bible School and preached in the main congregation.

I was equipping the saints for the work of the ministry. Thinking of myself as a warrior for God, I was ready for the challenge. As the youngest elder at age 25, I envisioned a Billy Graham-style ministry by the time I reached 30. (I would have done well to memorize Proverbs 11:2, *"When pride cometh, then cometh shame, but with the lowly is wisdom."*)

We quickly formed teams to blanket the city. Trusting the Holy Spirit to lead, we witnessed on street corners, went door to door, invaded rock concerts and picked up hitchhikers. We also targeted prostitutes, drug addicts, drunks, homosexuals, and thieves. Twice, hundreds of church members marched through downtown, proclaiming Jesus and handing out tracts, which brought plenty of media attention.

In addition, I handled much of the work of a pastor, counseling with many people and officiating at thirty weddings my first fifteen months. Midway through the second year, I went to see Joseph Woods.

"Brother, I would like to take a team and start a new church in Atlanta, Georgia," I smiled. "I feel led to go back to the city where I grew up as a teenager and pastor a New Testament Church.

He didn't say much, but with a look of surprise he cleared his throat, "Well...I'll bring it up for discussion at the next elders' meeting."

The elders weren't too receptive, particularly because of my age and lack of experience. In response, I persisted and persuaded.

"I'm ready to leave the warmth and security of this great church. My mother church has been good to me, but it's time for this young eagle to fly. I KNOW I can fly. I KNOW the Bible. I KNOW the principles of faith. I KNOW the answers to life's questions. I KNOW God has destined me for greatness in the ministry. My church will probably grow to 1,000 within the first year." *Obviously what I didn't KNOW was humility.*

It took three meetings before I convinced them, although their picture of unified support for my dream of a new church in Atlanta hung in a frame of reluctance.

The news was advertised in the church bulletin and 30 people came forward to announce their intentions of moving south to be the founding members of the Atlanta Christian Center.

6

TROUBLE IN ATLANTA

"If a preacher committed adultery in a moment of weakness, would God forgive him?"

Casually toying with the edge of her bathrobe, the attractive 22-year-old woman smiled seductively, looking up from the floor and dripping honey into my eyes. I had gone to her home on the assumption I would counsel her with her mother present. Once inside, she told me, "Something came up and my mother had to visit someone."

Quickly her conversation became explicit, and thanks to my previous training on this subject, a one-word warning flashed through my brain: run!

"When your mother gets home," I said as I hastily stood up, "have her give me a call." As I drove away from the house, a sense of warmth flowed over me. I praised the Lord for the power to overcome. In Genesis 39, Joseph fled from an adulterous invitation from Potiphar's wife. Now I had passed a similar test.

Given my careful practice in Anchorage to avoid all appearance of evil and hug only grandmotherly types, I never dreamed that sexual temptation would ensnare me in Atlanta.

Pride in our own power is an invitation to trouble. Of course, trouble never sneaks up the alley behind the house. He parks out front and strolls up to the door so casually you never suspect that an enemy is knocking. So, it's not surprising that I never dreamed Satan would bait a trap in my own congregation. It came in the form of a 20-year-old woman who, along with her husband, became close friends before we moved.

In Atlanta, we took up residence in the same condominium complex near the church and grew closer. Cathy talked with Rose almost daily and they often went shopping together, sharing their innermost thoughts.

"You know, Cathy's been having fantasies about you," Rose laughed one day when they returned from the mall.

Surprised that my wife would even tell me about her best friend's daydreams, I urged, "Rose, you need to exhort her. Counsel her from the Word. Tell her about the need for fidelity in marriage."

Instead, two weeks later, Rose came home and announced, "Cathy's been having carnal dreams about you lately."

I frowned. "Listen, Rose, do whatever is necessary to get the situation under control."

But inwardly, I entertained fantasies about Cathy. Like a foolish moth enticed by a flickering flame, I began wondering what it would be like if I ever found myself with a "secret" opportunity to make Cathy's dreams come true.

The Atlanta Christian Center held its opening services on the nation's 200th birthday in 1976, and the 30 Alaskans who attended that inaugural ceremony were bursting with enthusiasm. For six months before moving, we met on a weekly basis for prayer and fellowship, often discussing our plans and goals. We claimed that within a year the church would mushroom to 1,000 members, start a large orchestra, and excel in praise and worship. We were determined to become a shining example of a balanced New Testament church.

Slowly, reality set in. Although we had purchased an old Baptist church building on a two-acre site, it would take a miracle for our congregation to touch the 1,000 mark. By the end of nine months, services averaged just fifty people and our largest single-Sunday attendance had been one hundred. Our image of dynamic growth and charismatic excitement dissolved into boring reality.

As the tedium of building a fledgling organization set in, I gradually neglected the fundamentals of a sound Christian walk: prayer, Bible study, and close fellowship with other believers. The Lord had blessed me with preaching ability and I thought a little prayer and casual conversation were all I needed to carry on. How dumb and arrogant! As I tried to coast on my wave of fleshly strength, the lack of discipline allowed self deception to cloud my thinking. Instead of confessing the temptation that took root in my mind, I watered it. Even though my own marriage had blossomed into a mature relationship. Rose, was in every way a Godly woman, teaching the children at church and serving as a role model for her peers.

Despite my good training, lust tugged at me. Before I began living for the Lord, I had indulged myself with many women. Like most men I looked at my share of pornography. Contending with that background was challenge enough, but the lure of a willing companion proved insurmountable. Now in my late twenty's, a woman eight years younger looked so fresh with blonde hair sweeping over her shoulders. I was stunned by her beauty - helpless prey for her witty, entertaining personality.

As if I needed additional temptation, I foolishly accepted Cathy's offers of free secretarial assistance. One day to demonstrate my gratitude, I treated her to lunch at a posh restaurant in downtown Atlanta. Basking in the tantalizing, worldly atmosphere, I smiled broadly as Cathy fed my ego more skillfully than the chef fed us.

A week later, she reappeared at the church office, smiling as she bustled around in her customary helpful manner. At midmorning, she enticed me with a question, "Something's happening in my life and I can't tell anybody else about it...can you guess what it is?"

Instead of answering I said, "Well, that's funny. Something's going on with me that I can't tell anyone else about, either."

We finally quit flirting and I invited her into my lap. Our emotions exploded in passion, fueled by the anticipation that had simmered over a nine-month-long flame. Soon, we decided to take a drive to "talk things over." When we reached the country, all inhibitions vanished.

My emotions swirled in a pool of confusion. Guilt washed over me and I knew every time I tried to preach that Conscience would be sitting on my shoulder, reminding me of unresolved problems. But lust kept whispering,

"Wasn't that great? She loves you!"

Losing The Battle

Following this episode, I tried preaching one more time. I shared with the congregation an appropriate message for myself, "We may lose battles, but it doesn't mean we have lost the war. Keep going and ultimately we will win."

My unconvincing, halting, and sometimes distracted delivery tipped off a good friend. Sensing I had a problem, my associate pastor asked after the service if there was anything he could do to help. Stone-faced, I brushed him off with an evasive remark.

"I can work it out. I appreciate your offer, but I need to work it out for myself."

Instead, a few days later Cathy and I hopped a jet for the Bahamas. Burdened by a mixture of guilt and the deceitful lure of sin, we gave in to the lust of the flesh and escaped from reality. Our trip to "Fantasy Island" lasted ten days, the limit of our ability to enjoy loafing on the beach and partying.

Cathy and I reached a mutual decision to return to Atlanta. The ugliness and severity of our behavior clouded our thinking, but we knew our money wouldn't last forever. Unpleasant as it would be, we had to go back and attempt to deal with the pain and emotional damage we had inflicted on dozens of people.

My character had been tested again. Only this

time I had failed miserably. I betrayed my wife, my children, my church and most of all, my Savior, Jesus Christ. I had trespassed against man and sinned against God. I deserved God's judgment.

Rose met me at the airport, a soldier summoning every ounce of her strength. Holding me in her arms, she told me she understood and that everything would be all right. Both of us were in shock as we waded through the motions of coping, all the time feeling like we were sleepwalking through a bad dream.

A friend had reserved a hotel room for us to spend some time alone, and there I begged for understanding.

"Rose, I love you very much, and I would like to continue our marriage. I realize what I've done is sick and disgusting and I don't deserve any mercy, but I'm asking you to forgive me and take me back as your husband."

Teardrops trickling down her cheeks, she smiled, "I forgive you...and I will love you forever."

As we silently embraced for what seemed like hours, I thanked God for His mercy, asked Him for strength and prayed for His forgiveness. With faith, I tried to receive His forgiveness, but experienced little peace as I drifted off to sleep.

When I awoke, a realization of the shame and guilt of my condition overwhelmed me. Both God and Rose had forgiven me, but I still had to face my children, my friends, and the congregation.

I did not feel forgiven.

Trained to be strong and to walk with dignity, instead I felt defeated, insecure, afraid, and drained of every shred of self-respect.

"Curtis, you know I have to leave," I told the associate pastor that afternoon as I packed my books. "I've talked with some people I'm close to so they'll know what's going on, but...I just can't handle the rest. I can't face everyone. God's people have been abused. And I'm the abuser. Please ask them to forgive me."

At home, my children ran to me with open arms when I opened the door. We hugged, kissed, and reaffirmed our love for each other. I cared for them so much. How could I have done such a terrible thing?

Conditional Forgiveness

"How could you!!!???" Rose and I were laying in bed that evening, sighing as we struggled to talk, when she suddenly broke down.

"How could you?" she screamed. "How could you just wreck our life? How could you destroy everything we had!"

I frowned, trying to maintain my calm, and nodded, "I know."

"I liked being a pastor's wife," she continued, tears flowing in a steady stream, "and I was starting to feel secure in ministering to the ladies. Now that's all over."

"I blew it and I realize you don't deserve what is happening," I replied. "But this is reality. I feel bad. The truth is I'm weak. I want to keep trying, but I need your support. If you continue to condemn and remind me of my failure, it's going to be very difficult to recover."

"What kind of sexual fantasies did you fulfill with Cathy?!" she screamed back. "You guys had your fun and now you're back. After shattering my life!"

"I don't want to talk about it anymore. I know I did wrong. I love you. There is nothing else to be said. Please, let's go to sleep."

Rose cried herself into a state of exhaustion. As I brooded over the future, fear crawled in under the covers and snuggled up next to me.

The next day brought an unexpected call from a visiting friend. We had known each other in Alaska and he now pastored a church in Colorado. Hoping to receive some encouragement, I eagerly accepted his dinner invitation. Words have the power of life and death, and after all the daggers that had been flying, I frantically sought some healing. Still an emotional wreck, Rose reluctantly agreed to go.

The opening greetings were pleasant, but as soon as the waitress had gathered up our menus, he launched his attack.

"How could you have done what you did?"

"I failed," I shrugged. "I was tempted and I gave in. I'm not as strong as I thought I was."

His wife turned to Rose and very matter of factly asked "Doesn't this make you feel less than a woman?"

Rose cried throughout the rest of dinner.

Feeling it was their duty to rebuke me, they continued with legalistic, self-righteous pronouncements, amply laced with scripture. The rest of our meal tasted so cold it might as well have remained in the freezer.

Galatians 6:1 instructs believers to restore those overtaken by sin with meekness, but apparently they didn't know that verse.

The guilt, combined with frequent verbal condemnation, prevented the healing and restoration I so desperately needed. Rose needed immediate spiritual counseling and attention too, but none appeared.

Over the next week, my wife's attacks intensified as the spiritual warfare peaked. Already confused and hurt over the lack of understanding shown by most people, and angered by

Rose's "forgiveness" — a hollow act amidst her shower of criticism — I buckled. The pressure mounted, but in my selfishness, I wanted only comfort, kind words, help, and understanding. A week after we returned from our escapade, I dialed Cathy's number.

"It's not working with Rose and me and I can't handle this condemnation," I said. "You want to go?"

Like a dog returning to its vomit, we again hit the road, running from Florida all the way to California while we tried to escape from reality. As before, our fantasy world collapsed in a little over two weeks and meekly we returned to our mates.

Sex is a God-given gift, meant to be a unique form of sharing and communication between man and wife. It's also one of the strongest drives within humans, which is why Satan strives so hard to pervert it. There is within each one of us the ability to commit wanton acts if we allow that fleshly nature to be unlocked and give the devil an opportunity to "inspire" us. The power of sexual temptation is so awesome that unless you walk carefully on a Godly path and wisely resist this trap, it can destroy your life.

7
RUNNING

"How could you destroy our lives? Don't you love me? What about our children? Didn't you think about our future?"

"Rose, I..."

"What's wrong with you? Why are you such a pervert? You're so messed up."

"You know, Rose, we've been down here for a month and right now I'm at the end of my rope. It's not like you never did anything wrong. Or are you forgetting? Remember how you moved in with your old boyfriend? How you hooked up with one of my best friends? Half a dozen times?"

"That was years ago! That doesn't have anything to do with right now! I've got my act together. So what happened to you, preacher man?"

I didn't answer. Shaking my head, I stared

down Clearwater Beach and wondered how much more verbal abuse I could endure. Sending two of the children off to stay with our mothers, we had taken our youngest boy (and what little money remained after my escapades) and drove to Florida. We hoped to recuperate and achieve a reconciliation, but with constant battles straining the seams of our wounded marriage, the situation deteriorated.

During our first week in Florida, three ministers affiliated with our home church in Alaska flew down to see me. They were kind and willing, but despite their attempts to reach out I was unable to intelligently discuss many issues.

"I love God and I want to get it together," I told them at the end of our two-day session. "But I'm hurting. I think I'll be able to recover, though. I don't think it will be too long before I return to the ministry."

"Well, realistically it probably will be five years," one of them responded.

"Well," I mused, "I don't think it will take that long. But then, you could be right." I didn't feel like arguing with him.

Whenever you're in a high-profile position that carries a lot of responsibility, time is the great healer. Having lived through it, I believe a year is the absolute minimum needed to recover from the shame of public exposure of your sin. Granted, everybody stumbles, but not everyone lives in the spotlight. Nor must they overcome extreme embarrassment, humiliation, and incredible self-doubt to return to their job.

I was no longer trustworthy. It would take time to rebuild my life. But, I really believed I was willing to pay the price to regain the trust of my peers and my family.

Because I had submitted my life to the Lord and answered His call to preach, I mistakenly thought I was above fleshly temptations. In the aftermath of Atlanta, an awesome awareness of my weakness struck me harder than a bolt of lightning. I was nothing more than an ordinary mortal who had failed God, family, and church. The ugly depths of my human character had surfaced.

Rose's nagging made me feel worse. Her words hurt rather than angered, and plunged into my soul with the force of a double-edged sword. In a broken, fragile state herself, she seemed intent on snapping me in two. Thus, I chose a familiar route. Escape.

"Rose, I'm going to walk down the beach to watch these guys fishing," I said the afternoon of her latest tongue-lashing. Only I kept walking. Leaving the beach, I headed for the highway, where I hitchhiked to Daytona Beach and partied with college students for two weeks. When my limited means ran out, I hitched back to my mother's house in central Florida.

That was the beginning of a pattern that would finally end with heartache and division. More than once, we tried to make things work, but had always failed.

When I called Rose (who had flown back to Alaska) from my mother's house, she forgave me. Then, we agreed to enter a restoration program at Anchorage Community Church.

There, after being humbled and told the sin I committed ranked "worse than a heathen's," I experienced the pain of being treated like a leper. The church leadership proved to be untrained to provide the support, love, vision, and hope that both Rose and I needed. It takes a wise, mature ministry to counsel backsliders and their mates, but it seemed most people preferred punishment to restoration.

The attitude of the elders was like this, "Come to church, sit in your pew, pay your tithes, work hard and provide for your family while we watch you. In the meantime, don't try to do anything here. You're damaged goods and in your condition we can't have you praying with anyone."

So I went to work, setting up shop as a painting contractor and making a good living. However, after three months of serving as an outcast, I sought a private meeting with Joseph Woods my spiritual father and founder of Anchorage Community Church.

"Look, I'm hurting," I explained, trying to maintain my composure. "I haven't had any fellowship in a long time. You've got to remember that for years I had daily contact with a lot of Christian people. Now I feel like an outsider. I come to church but I don't feel a part of it because I can't participate. I need some joy in my life, I need some encouragement."

Despite his promise to talk with the elders and my own impassioned plea, no hospitality emerged. Three more months passed before frustration took its toll. None of the 30 elders of my Church had yet asked me out for lunch or out for coffee and fellowship. One afternoon I bought a half-pint of brandy (my first brush with alcohol since returning to Anchorage) and drove to the top of a mountain overlooking the city. Silently, I drowned my sorrows.

"I'm sorry, God," I mumbled through half-drunken tears after draining the bottle. "I just can't take any more. Nobody wants anything to do with me. I'm lonely and the pain is too much for me to bear. I can't handle it anymore."

When I ran this time, it was for a six-week vacation in Hawaii, where I survived by working in the lucrative marijuana trade, buying pot and reselling it to tourists for twice my price.

Working two hours a day, I averaged a daily profit of $100, which more than covered the rent for my cheap motel room in Waikiki.

Six months later, I returned for another six-week stay. In the meantime, I went back to Anchorage, resumed my painting career and dropped out of church. Initially, our marriage improved. Freed from the bondage of living up to the expectations of others, we found ourselves more relaxed. But, finally the combination of my slowly-increasing drinking habit and Rose's nagging sent me back to the airport.

After my second sojourn in Hawaii, I flew to Las Vegas, where I gambled away my last couple hundred dollars before hitchhiking back to Atlanta with a nickel in my pocket.

En route to Georgia, a Christian book distributor gave me a fifty-mile ride in Tennessee. I appreciated his encouragement as much as the five-dollar bill he gave me for food. That seed of love (and many others) would bear fruit much later. Never underestimate the help you lend to a stumbling saint.

In Atlanta I visited the associate pastor who had filled the pulpit when I resigned, and wound up calling Joseph Woods from this pastor's home. Tearfully, I asked "can I move in with you and your family?"

"I'll pray about it and call you tomorrow" he sincerely responded. I neglected to tell him that even as we talked I was in the middle of an LSD trip.

I waited anxiously the next day until the phone finally rang.

"Mike, I'm sorry but I don't feel led to help you." I was hurt, but I knew I was receiving a dose of "tough love."

Leaving the city, I drove to Miami with a backsliding ex-member of Atlanta Christian Center.

Realizing that lust formed our only bond, I left her one day at the hotel and hitched twenty-five miles north to Fort Lauderdale.

There I stayed with a pastor from Anchorage who had founded a local church in the area. He encouraged me to fast and pray, three days later I called Rose.

"I've divorced you," she greeted me. "It only takes thirty days to get a divorce up here and you've been gone for more than two months. You're not wanted here, Michael. The church doesn't want you. I don't want you. Nobody wants you. Stay away."

"No, Rose, you don't understand. I've been fasting and God has encouraged me. He's forgiven me. I feel cleansed. Life will go on. Yes, I've blown it, but I can start over."

"No, you're not wanted."

"Well, I'm coming back and you and I are going to get married again," I smiled into the phone.

"No, we're not."

"Yes, we are."

And we were. In the first church we attended after turning our lives over to the Lord, with our children participating in the wedding and a large crowd of guests looking on. That started us back on the path to normalcy, as I reestablished myself as a painting contractor and soon had five men working with me.

But we failed to plant ourselves in a local congregation, though we visited many and were sincere about our desire to serve the Lord. James Smith, an old friend who was in town for a ministers' conference, resolved the situation by inviting us to move to Seattle and join his congregation. Rose and I realized there had to be a better way than wandering through life, so we agreed.

Seattle marked the final stop in our marriage.

Things fell apart quickly when the painting demand slacked off and I lost my union post a month after we moved there in mid-1978. Depression set in and soon I regularly visited the local card room, drinking and gambling away our scant resources.

As she watched me quickly sliding downhill, Rose entered a familiar stage of panic, wondering which would come first: our eviction or my disappearance. So when an old friend whom I had led to salvation (prior to his messy divorce) called, she didn't take long to consider his offer. During one of my disappearing acts they had carried on a short affair.

"I've talked with Ron," she said one afternoon when I walked in after another losing round at the card table. "He is offering me marriage and a future. He has a house, a boat, and a good job....I love you, Mike, but I've got to be concerned about my future, about our kids' future."

Tears misted over her eyes and started trickling down her cheeks. "You are so messed up," momentarily deflecting her sobs. "I can't live like this. I can't take any more. I am going to take him up on it. I need some rest. I need some security. Most of all, I need some peace."

Pain flowed through my soul as the truth of her words stabbed at me. I loved her deeply, but somehow I couldn't summon the courage to be responsible. My life had again veered out of control.

"Well, I understand," I sighed. "I'm messed up and you do need what you're talking about. Obviously, I'm not providing enough for you. so, I don't blame you."

I thought back over my unstable past, the years of moving around and how I accepted that instability as a normal pattern of life. Now was no time to be passing blame. I had created this mess.

However, that didn't ease the hurt. The day I drove Rose to the airport, I cried all the way home. This had to be a bad dream. If only I could wake up and make it all disappear!

"I guess I'm just a loser," I thought as I pulled up in front of our now-empty home.

I returned to church the following Sunday morning for the final time. Sitting there alone in a pew and watching couples share little hugs or knowing smiles. After the service as I watched parents playing with their children, I felt so alone the emotional cauldron inside me boiled over. I knew I couldn't survive in this atmosphere. My despair was deep and it was time to run again.

Right before I left Seattle, our associate pastor asked what I planned to do.

"Well, realistically, Rose is getting a divorce, so I'll be divorced. But I will continue to believe in God and trust that He will help me get my act together. Of course, I knew that unless I got my head together with Jesus nothing was going to work out.

A week later, I headed south on Interstate 5

in my Chrysler Lebaron. Drinking and gambling rated higher than restoration on my priority list. But when you're not thinking clearly, it's easy to invent a million excuses for carrying on with your sin.

8
RESTORATION DENIED

A little bad luck tossing dice, too few winners at the blackjack tables and some drinks to chase away the gloom of losing, and the small wad of cash I had carried to Lake Tahoe evaporated. I decided to sleep in my car for a couple of nights, but the next afternoon walked into the Good News Church. I approached a man who looked like the pastor.

"Huh, you got a minute?"

"Certainly," the pastor said. "How can I help?"

"Right now," I grimaced, staring at the floor, "I could use a place to stay."

After I related my background, he informed me about their rooming house, which they maintained as an outreach to single men. Since the other four residents were in their early twenties, I quickly fit in as a type of older brother.

In hopes of finding the spiritual rudder that had been missing from my life for more than a year, I also began attending services at the 150-member church.

Good News proved to be just that. Friendly and interdenominational, a young, energetic congregation populated the praise-filled temple. But in my lonely condition, the most exciting attraction proved to be Shelley, an unattached, attractive divorcee about my age. I approached her after a Sunday night service and asked if she wanted to enjoy some Christian fellowship at the restaurant across the street.

"Your wife left you?" she said, eyebrows raising after we had made it through the routine introductions and recitations of how we ended up in Lake Tahoe. "What is it with people today? Doesn't anyone know how to be faithful?" I probably didn't tell her about the many times I left Rose and the many crisis I put her through.

"You too?" I asked.

"Me too," she shook her head. "Sometimes I just don't understand. It's not as if I were that unattractive or never paid any attention to him...."

We shared about the miseries of life we had experienced, when Shelley suddenly paused. She looked at me silently, her eyes searching my face.

"But, then, if this is what it took for us to meet..."

Already Engaged

"Hey, man, it's after 1 o'clock," grinned my buddy who had waited up to hear about my "date" when I finally came in. "You two hit it off?"

"Well...lll..lll..."

"Well? Well what, man?"

"Well," I grinned, "we're engaged."

"NO!!"

"Yeah. We talked nonstop for four hours and agreed that we're pretty compatible."

"Naw," he giggled, then started laughing and running his hands through his hair, shaking from side to side.

"It is pretty crazy," I grinned.

So, after entering the Lake Tahoe church in the lowly position of asking for a place to live, three months later I floated on cloud nine. I purchased our wedding rings and her mother agreed to sew a wedding dress. I found steady work, my self-esteem rose dramatically and I felt my relationship with the Lord growing deeper and more solid.

Since past setbacks had ruined my dreams more than once, I tried to focus on living a day at a time. But as I contemplated a future with a beautiful lady...especially one who cared so much about me...I wondered how things could go wrong. God had blessed me in spite of all my failures!

That's when the letter arrived. James Smith, my former friend and pastor from Seattle, learned of my whereabouts.

"The elders of this church and I have decided that you need discipline and judgment," Smith's letter began. "Therefore we are going to excommunicate you and cast you into the hands of the devil so that you can learn your lesson."

When I finished reading, I prayed for divine wisdom and inspiration, and slowly crafted a response.

"I realize that I've offended you, hurt you, and disappointed you," I wrote. "I would like to ask you to forgive me for anything that I've done. I've asked God to forgive me and He has. I'm trying to get my life together now. I'm no longer part of your church or Anchorage Community Church. I'm in a new church, starting over, and hope we can resolve this."

They sent a tersely-worded reply, informing me they were proceeding with the excommunication and inviting me to the official meeting which would be held in Anchorage. Thinking they would act more rationally if I could see them in person and explain, I made plans to attend. Terry, my current pastor, agreed to come as a character witness. He was prepared to testify that as far as he knew I was not causing any problems in his church. I attended three services a week and was always early for prayer. I was being healed and my restoration was coming along at a reasonable pace.

It turned out we should have saved our plane fare. Goaded by Smith, who nursed a grudge for my failures in Seattle, the elders and leaders believed I was guilty of more than I had done. My sins were shameful enough without my ex-pastor exaggerating the facts. I confessed to all their accusations except for the one about a planned premeditated scheme to drive Rose away so I could be freed of her. Rose testified at the meeting that she did not believe that I intended to drive her away. It didn't matter. They already knew what decision they were going to make.

"This Church and you leaders taught me that if I confess my sin and ask God to forgive me then He will. I've asked God to forgive me and He has, now I'm asking you to forgive me," I sincerely pleaded.

Pastor Smith did a thorough job of setting

me up. He convinced these men of God that I was unable to even distinguish between right and wrong, therefore I couldn't biblically repent because of my deranged mental state.

Joseph Woods didn't take the time to interview me one on one before the official meeting. He made a decision to accept the evaluation of my condition that was given to him by Pastor Smith and Smith's elders in Seattle. I believe that if he had only talked to me he would have known that excommunication was not necessary. Three months had passed since I had been part of their fellowship. I was starting over in a new denomination and yet somehow these things were overlooked.

After many rebukes, and an overdose of humiliation, Joseph Woods pronounced my judgment, "Mike Premo, it is with much sorrow that we excommunicate you from the Church. We deliver you into the hands of Satan for the destruction of your flesh. We pray that your soul will be saved in the day of the Lord Jesus."

Then his associate pastor added "Our hope is that not one church in the world would open their doors to you for fellowship."

Feeling rejected and misunderstood old feelings immediately surfaced. I again chose flight over standing in the face of turmoil.

"Shelley, it's over," I said that night when I

called Lake Tahoe. "They've gone through with it. The church has excommunicated me and now I'm really messed up."

"We can make it," she insisted through her tears. "Don't give up, Mike. I need you."

"You don't know about these things," I said, hating myself for walking away. "I'm messed up and it's going to take me awhile to get over this. I'm sorry, but I need out."

Beaten Down

"Your hair is weird," said the Eskimo woman as she climbed into my cab, her liquor-stained breath curling my nostrils. "Why don't you comb it?"

"Because I don't have anybody to comb it for."

"You've let them beat you," she grunted.

In the rear-view mirror, I could see her slowly shaking her head.

"Why did you let them beat you?" she asked.

Tightening my lips, I drove on. What could I say? Fighting the flu while I drove a cab twelve hours a day, with no wife or kids to come home to at the end of a long shift — right now I felt like a loser. As if I needed additional discouragement, my excommunication assured that no one from my old church would talk to me, either. What kind of life was this?

I had become a cabbie after returning to Anchorage. My escape from everything and everyone who could hurt me had been a long road:

Two weeks of playing golf in southern California...a few days in Las Vegas, where I stole a billfold with enough money to fly to Hawaii...where the police caught me with stolen traveler's checks and proceeded to throw me into a hotel bathroom and beat me until my clothes were bloody from their kicks and punches.

"Are you ready to die?" they asked trying to intimidate me into giving a full confession.

"Actually I don't have a whole lot going for me at this time in my life so I really don't care," I responded. After a couple of days in jail they had to let me go because they had failed to get the proper search warrant...but not before they threatened to pound my face every time they saw me on the beach...then quickly hopping a plane back to Anchorage.

Before the authorities in Hawaii unexpectedly released me, I had talked with God. "Well, Lord, if this is what it takes, this is what it takes. Go for it. While I'm in jail, I'll have a lot of time to get my head together, do a lot of reading without a lot of pressure. I'll get my act together in jail if that's the way it has to be." I knew

God had not forsaken me in spite of my sin and self-pity.

Then He intervened. Maybe that overwhelming instance of grace impressed me more than I knew. Or maybe I realized that He was speaking through that Eskimo woman, telling me if I lost my vision, then I certainly would perish. Whatever the reason, soon after I wound up preaching in a most unlikely setting: sniffing cocaine outside a bar.

God Is Great

I unexpectedly saw a group of backsliders from Anchorage Community Church at the bar and we stepped out for a "snort." Because of our past association, the conversation inevitably turned to spiritual topics.

"Hey, we're backsliding, but that has nothing to do with who God is," I said. "God is good, God is great. He's fantastic."

Dave, an old friend who had played in the J.C. & Company band in the early seventies, argued that the church was deceived and that the gifts of the Holy Spirit were a hoax, invented by phony Christians.

"No," I said. "It's not that way at all. It's all real. It's all right on. Yeah, the Church isn't perfect and some things that go on aren't always led by God, but the fact is we're the one's messed up. We're in rebellion. We're doing our own thing, but that has nothing to do with them or God. We're sinning and running."

"Well, we might as well sin it up. Better to have some fun than act like that bunch of hypocrites," he sneered.

Despite Dave's continuous badgering and attempts at sowing confusion, I delivered a salvation message. One of the men who worked as a chef proved to be my primary audience. I told him about Jesus' crucifixion, the basic plan of salvation and how the purpose of life lay in serving God, giving all our desires over to Him, and being productive in spreading the gospel.

After Dave interrupted for the third or fourth time, the chef turned and poked a finger in his direction: "Hey, I want you to be quiet. I'm listening to what Mike is saying and what he's saying is making sense to me. I want him to continue."

"So that's the purpose of life," I continued, "to serve God. But our flesh is weak. It wants to rebel and live it up, have a good time or escape from responsibility and medicate the pain of life through alcohol and drug abuse. That's where we're at. I believe in God but I'm not living it because I'm having a pity party. I've gone through a divorce, my old church excommunicated me, and I don't have my kids anymore. Bad things are happening.

"So I'm feeling sorry for myself and right now I'm getting stoned. One of these days I'm going to get it back together because what I'm telling you is real. God is love. I'm too messed up right now and too weak to get my head together. But I will get back into church eventually."

However, taking that step would require one more shock to my system. It occurred after I had drifted back to a familiar scene in Lake Tahoe. While I wasted time playing craps and drinking, I planned on how I would use the hotel room key I had kept after my last visit to the city.

The hotel housed one of the nicer casinos on the strip. I figured I could slip into my old room, grab the valuables of the people there while they were gambling, and slip out.

"Aha," I thought after closing the door, "a purse, which means a wallet. And lots of cash for the crap table."

Squeak!

My heart leaped. Before I could even pick up the purse, I heard the key go into the doorknob.

I frantically glanced around. I couldn't open the windows, nor would I have wanted to take a dive off the ninth floor. Trying to turn invisible, I slid behind the door as a nicely-dressed blonde in her mid-twenties pushed it open, fiddling with the key. Momentarily freezing when she felt my feet blocking the door, she gasped, then turned and dashed into the hallway.

"Help! Help! There's a man in my room! Somebody help!"

Trying to maintain my composure, I called on my old burglary training. Quickly inventing an excuse for my presence, I cleared my throat, stepped from behind the door and casually walked outside.

"Ma'am, I'm the hotel electrician and I was just working on your TV set," I said. "It's working fine now, there's no problem. You can go back to your room."

She stared at me in disbelief.

Realizing she thought a potential rapist stood before her, I casually walked toward the elevator, knowing she would run elsewhere. She scurried back to her room, and I jumped into action, knowing she would pick up the phone, call the front desk and have security guards swarming throughout the hotel.

Guessing I had no more than two minutes, when the elevator car reached the lobby I hurriedly paced through the casino, trying not to attract any attention. In the parking lot, I broke into a dead run, hurdled a fence, and scooted across the adjoining Edgewood Golf Course. Ribs heaving when I reached my own hotel, I slipped inside and collapsed on my bed, my veins throbbing with a mixture of nervous adrenaline and fright. I had come within moments of a return trip to prison.

Regret gnawed at me, too. The impact of seeing that young lady's face pierced my conscience. She looked like the kind of woman who had been raised in a nice, middle-class home, and who had suddenly come eyeball-to-eyeball with crime and devastation. Without warning, I had intruded in her world. It didn't take much imagination to envision her being paranoid for the rest of her life.

"God," I sighed, looking at the ceiling, "I'm getting too old for this kind of lifestyle. This is wearing me out. I don't like the idea of hurting people. Help me, Lord. I really need Your help. This is a lousy way to live."

9

RESTORATION ACHIEVED

"I wonder what that big white cross is about?" I mused as I slowly drove down the Pacific Coast Highway. "It looks like a good place to break out my sleeping bag. If nothing else, there ought to be a powerful ocean view at the top."

I had spotted the cross after reaching Big Sur on the California coast, two hours south of San Francisco. I chose this scenic stretch of coastline as my destination after waking in Lake Tahoe, still sweating from my narrow escape. I had to surrender to God. Although I had never been there, I had read about Big Sur and thought it would offer a serene setting for a talk with the Lord as I sought His direction for my tattered life.

I flung my last carton of cigarettes in the dumpster of my Tahoe hotel, and headed west in an old Pinto with twenty dollars in my pocket. That would be just enough to buy gas for the 275-mile trip and a meager lunch.

During the leisurely trip, I worshipped the Lord, often lifting one hand from the steering wheel in praise.

"Lord, I'm doing it," I smiled, soothed by the thought of His renewed guidance over my life. "I'm putting my life in your hands. I don't know where I'm going or what I'm going to do, but here goes...by faith. This is the adventure."

Twilight had settled over the coast by the time the "Big Sur" signs greeted me. A huge white cross up on a hill overlooking the ocean jumped into sight, pulling me up the small, curving road leading to it. At the top, a Catholic monastery stood in the distance, nestled below the cross.

As I pulled to a stop, a monk emerged from the doorway.

"My name...Gabriel," he said in a slightly broken accent, extending his hand. "How may I help...you?"

"Yeah, I got a sleeping bag and I was wondering if I could sleep on the grass?"

"Well, we have guest quarters. You can stay here, have dinner with us tonight. In the morning, we send you on your way with breakfast."

"Praise God!" I thought. "He has already provided."

Over a meal of hot soup and homemade rolls, Gabriel described how he had spent 14 years on this mountain, seeking the Lord. When he finished, he asked, "Are you Christian, Mike?"

"Well, yes, I am and I've just rededicated my life to God today."

"Wonderful," he said, slowly rubbing his hands together. "I want to take you into my prayer room and pray with you."

As soon as we walked inside, he raised his hands as he enthusiastically praised the Lord. That struck me as a little unusual for a Catholic, but I lifted my hands with him. Soon we kneeled to pray and he began speaking in tongues...a charismatic monk!

"I feel to lay hands on you and pray for you," he said. When his hands touched my shoulders he began prophesying, "Thus saith the Lord, 'God has called you to preach the Good News and to proclaim the acceptable year of the Lord, to set the captives free and to heal the sick'...."

I can't specifically remember the rest of Gabriel's message, but something so positive, encouraging, faith-filled, and uplifting that I knew it to be a gift from the Lord. At that moment, its value surpassed any riches the world could offer, and reinforced my desire to surrender to God.

The next morning, Gabriel handed me thirty-five dollars as we walked to my car: "Here, the Lord told me to give this to you."

Melodyland

Thanks to Gabriel's gift, I made it to Los Angeles, where some very good friends of mine lived. I knew Carl and Joanne Gove from Alaska; and in my times of need they were always willing to help me in any way they could. They put me up and ministered valid Christian love to me until I decided what I was going to do.

I planned to visit the famed Melodyland Christian Center, across from Disneyland in Anaheim.

Pastor Ralph Wilkerson had been quite kind during my California visit in 1973 to surrender for my probation violations. At a prayer breakfast at the church, he invited me to share my testimony, then unexpectedly took up an offering which enabled us to pay our rent (which "happened" to be due the next day).

After a brief visit, I checked in at Melodyland's drug crisis department and arranged to stay at their Christian halfway house. My living quarters would cost fifty dollars a week, but not until I found a job.

At the time the church's congregation numbered in the thousands. In addition to a variety of ministries, they hosted an annual Charismatic Clinic featuring preachers from around the world. The week I moved into the halfway house coincided with the 1980 clinic.

Desperately needing strengthening and encouragement, I felt quite blessed to be able to attend the clinic. However, I never expected the prophetic word that Dick Mills - an experienced, widely-traveled evangelist - delivered.

"I'd like for the young man in the back with the blue sweater to stand up," he said when he finished teaching. "I have a word from God for you."

Nervously, I obeyed.

"Within ninty days great and mighty things are going to happen in your life," he said, backing up his message with several scriptures.

"I've lost everything," I grinned after the service, "but now I have everything in life because my life is back in God's will. I'm not going to run anymore."

Sweet Sue

"You're from Alaska?"

Hearing the evangelist asking me about my home church, an attractive, brown-eyed brunette with a captivating smile approached me after his message.

"Yes."

"I know some people from there and I was wondering if you might know them," she said, ticking off names of people who had attended Anchorage Community's Bible school when I taught there. After we exchanged names, Sue gave me a funny look; I could tell by the expression on her face she had heard of me. As I would later discover, she worked for the same freight airline as a friend of mine. He had told her about a preacher who once was used of God and then backslid. After my friend finished my story, Sue - with compassion filling her heart - felt moved to pray for a fallen preacher even though she had never met me.

"Well, maybe this is God's gift for me," I thought as we talked with the ease of friends reunited after a long absence. We went out for coffee that day and the next, attended the rest of the seminar together, and became as well acquainted in two weeks as time permitted.

It didn't take long before I told Sue, "I believe it's God's will that we get married."

My impulsive statement shocked her! Saved two years earlier, her constant prayers included a request that the Lord unite her with an evangelist. But at the moment, my qualifications were expired. Staring back, she replied, "Well, I'm going to have to pray about it."

After she returned to her home in Seattle, she corresponded with me for another two weeks before she accepted my proposal. To my delight I received daily love letters mixed with sensitive spiritual encouragement. Her letters imparted strength, vision, and healing into my spirit. She was kinder than I deserved. She was a woman of God.

When a single, never-married female in her early thirties prepares to take the plunge, word circulates quickly. It traveled through her church until it reached an older couple who had been serving as her spiritual parents, who helped train her in her Christian walk.

"Who is he?" the woman smiled after Sue confirmed the news. But, when she heard my name, she dissolved into tears.

"Mike was engaged to our daughter."

This was the mother who had been preparing a wedding dress for Shelley...whom I had deserted in Lake Tahoe!

"Has he been restored?" she asked when her tears stopped.

"Yes," Sue said, defensibly, "he has gotten his head together now."

Sue could have answered that question truthfully, for during that same week James Smith, learning of my presence at Melodyland, had flown down to see me. After some discomforting discussion, he admitted to having exaggerated some of the details during my excommunication hearing and promised to report that I had since come back to the Lord. Nine months after being drummed out of the Anchorage

Community fellowship of churches, I was officially restored to fellowship.

Sue and I were married in November of 1980. My friend and pastor, James Smith officiated the wedding. We exchanged vows..."to love and cherish each other through the good times and the bad times..." Sue looked beautiful in her stunning white dress as her parents, six brothers and sister looked on with joy. My good friend Mark DeBenedetti was my best man and afterwards he dropped us off at our honeymoon suite.

I shared my heart with my new bride. "Sweet Sue, our marriage must be built upon the teachings of the Bible if it's going to be successful. As your husband I am charged by God to love and honor you. I do love and honor you, but there will be times that I will fall short of this responsibility, When I fail please have patience and pray for me.

My love will grow as time passes. When I fail hopefully I will confess my fault and continue in my commitment to always love you." I continued, "The Bible teaches that you as my wife are commanded to submit to me as unto the Lord. I realize that this charge will be very hard at times for you to practice. Nevertheless I expect you to believe that this is your responsibility if our marriage is going to have divine order. When you fail to submit to me I will try to be patient and understanding. Of course if I ever ask you to do something that is not bibically sound you are not bound to obey me. I believe God will establish our marriage as we honor Him and follow the Bible."

My Beautiful Gift from God!

Though lacking any formal status, I exhorted many people at church and in social gatherings. Encouraging God's people to witness, love and be open to the Holy Spirit's direction, I experienced the Lord's grace. He resurrected for service a confused sinner whom most people would have assigned to the spiritual scrap heap.

Besides exhorting the believers at our church, I started ministering in a downtown mission. There I counseled one night with a man who came forward to receive Christ and I asked, "Are you serious about God?"

"Yeah."

"Well, would you like to leave this mission and move in with my wife and me?"

"For sure man!"

"Is there anyone else you know who is serious about God?"

"That guy over there."

Walking over to the second man, I said, "Are you serious about following Jesus?"

After he nodded, I told him to pack his bags so he could move in with us. In the twinkling of an eye, two down-and-outers were bunking with Sue and I in our two-bedroom apartment.

That chance encounter formed the beginnings of "The Salvation Station." When our desires to help other men outgrew our accommodations, we moved into a large house and wound up with five boarders. The church helped to pay for their rent and food, while we set out to guide them in the Word and help them find work and become productive members of society. We wanted to give them an opportunity. They needed healing without condemnation. They had already faced plenty of that.

Why bother?

The value of reaching out to a "nobody" is best demonstrated by the life of the man who, at the age of thirty-five, had never held a driver's license. I invited him to leave the Rescue Mission and move in with Sue and I in 1982. He went on to secure a job at the Boeing aircraft plant and marry a sweet lady in our church. He quit using drugs and ever since has been a faithful member of that church in Seattle.

Re-Ordained

My zeal and tangible soul-winning efforts convinced a sometimes skeptical James Smith that the Lord had reached down inside my heart. In the late spring of 1982, the church re-ordained me as an evangelist.

I preached twice a month in the church and led numerous witnessing missions through the streets of Seattle. Knocking on doors and plunging into the streets, our salvation teams led people to Christ. In addition, I trained future evangelists from the church body and taught evangelism classes.

Six months after my ordination, Anchorage Community Church asked me to speak there one weekend. I could hardly believe it. "The prodigal son is returning home," I thought. "I'm blessed and obviously I don't deserve it. But it's happening anyway."

At that special service in early 1983 I spoke on "The Restoration of Evangelism," drawing my text from the Great Commission delivered by Jesus at the end of Matthew 28. I challenged, provoked, inspired, and encouraged, "the church has neglected evangelism, could we please consider telling people about JESUS."

"The church is not doing what Christ commanded," I preached. "Too many times, in too many places, the church is just ministering to itself. We have our fellowships, eat our food, do our thing and get rich, believing prosperity is our reason for living with our comfortable house and white picket fence. But the world is not being evangelized. We need to be restored to our Lord's vision, the fields are ready to be harvested, but the laborers are few. Let's forget about what we can get from God and instead seek out what we can give away.

Let's aim our desires at spiritual rewards instead of material. The world is dying. We need to introduce them to the Savior who offers eternal life."

The offer came within a week leaving me speechless and greatly honored.

Joseph Woods, who had called my life a blasphemy several years earlier now was offering complete restoration.

"Michael, we want you to join the staff here," he smiled when our session had ended. "We'll provide you with a good salary, your own office, and a parsonage with all utilities paid."

It was a miracle, this prodigal son came home and Joseph Woods my spiritual father cried as he restored his love and embraced me back into his heart.

PART THREE: TUMBLING DOWN

10

BAITING THE TRAP

Before we returned to Anchorage, Satan had begun baiting the trap, but I failed to recognize the same game that had ruined me in Atlanta. When I called from Seattle to talk to my children, Rose and I would also talk about the good times we used to have.

This temptation cropped up in the midst of my efforts to rid myself of carnality. Two months before I knew we would be returning to Alaska, I started a thirty-seven-day, water-only fast and lost forty pounds. As I put God first in my life, I drew closer to Him. Part of me really wanted to follow hard after God. But, the other part of me was not ready to surrender to the righteousness of walking in the footsteps of Jesus. Spiritual warfare.

Whenever I went to pick up the children on visits, Rose would be very cordial. She divorced me because of my wild and crazy ways but she let me know that she still loved me. I too was still attracted to her even though I knew it was not right. We were both guilty of tempting each other.

I should have nipped this poison rose in the bud. A meeting with Sue, our pastor, and Rose and her husband to air the truth could have avoided potential problems. Merely discussing it would have acted as a check in our spirits.

Instead, I remained silent. When Rose started flirting, (I did my share of flirting also) I tried to laugh it off, saying, "I'll always appreciate you. You'll always be my friend and I'll always think good things about you. But we're done. We're married to other people now and it's all over between us."

It wasn't. I tried avoiding her by taking the kids out for ice cream, to the park or movies. She waited patiently and inevitably we wound up sitting in the living room, talking intimately while the kids ran in and out of the house. They knew our love hadn't faded, which created an even stranger scene.

Confusion Reigns

This placed me in the middle of a confusing battle. Though I knew an affair with Rose violated God's commandments, our status as former marriage partners helped me dream up justifications if it came to pass.

Our attraction burned a little warmer every time I went to visit my children over the months and I helped fan the flame. Instead of confessing to a fellow staff member or Christian friend, I again remained silent.

As this dilemma grew, I reckoned, "I'm in trouble. This is awkward, dangerous, difficult...but what do I do? It's a miracle that God even put me here. How do I get out of this mess?"

Answers were all around me. The same things I neglected before still begged for attention — honesty, the Word, fellowship, and prayer. Foolishly, I let pride slip through the door, thinking I could control the situation while it resolved itself.

It didn't. The first time, I deceived myself into thinking this "isolated incident" would never happen again. We both repented and didn't see each other for a month.

During that time, I somehow carried on with teaching my classes in evangelism and the Book of Acts. When I stood in front of my impressionable students, most in their early twenties, I strived to separate Jesus from my rebellious, dark side. (As Paul said, "we preach Christ, not ourselves.")

Inwardly, I argued, "Yes, I'm weak and I have failed. But Christ is Christ and God is God. He's great, He's good, He's fantastic. I'm not preaching Mike Premo as the standard, I'm preaching Jesus. Look to Him, not me, because if you look at me or any other man you're going to be disappointed."

A month passed between our first and second liaison, but only a week between our second and third. I repented twice more before recognizing that I wouldn't be able to conquer this problem. Since she wasn't going anywhere, it became obvious I would have to remove myself.

During a vacation in Florida, Sue detected the danger signs. Though I preached in several churches in the south, I maintained the distance that my guilt had injected into our relationship. One night at a hotel I ordered some wine, mumbling, "I need this." I stopped after one glass, but that drink symbolized my predicament. I was leaning on the arm of flesh!

After our trip, the facade quickly fell. Without knowing about the affair, people recognized its consequences. The fire that once marked my leadership of church evangelism teams had evaporated into lukewarm tones of casual fellowship. Many had noticed, including the church staff.

Upon our return, Woods unveiled a plan during a staff meeting. He proposed I take six months off to work on maintenance and construction projects while mentally regrouping.

"Well, I may need to do something different," I sidestepped in my best deadpan expression. "There are some areas in my life that are lacking and I need to examine them and get it together."

I calmly walked out of the meeting with one thought in mind: leaving town. If I told the truth about the source of my discontent, no hope existed. Either way I was a goner, but by taking off I could avoid the shame and humiliation of telling the church I had disappointed them the second time.

Flight Pattern

As badly as I wanted to get my life together, I saw no way of achieving that goal. Sin controlled me. Better to run with the sin than take any more feeble stabs at fighting it, and save myself embarrassment in the process. After the meeting, I drove to Rose's house and told her what had happened.

The next day I packed a suitcase and started driving east for a few hours, stopped, and called Rose. "Listen, I'm in Tok, on the AlCan Highway, and I'm heading for L.A. I'm leaving."

"No, Mike, not again," tears starting to choke her voice. "Don't run."

"I can't talk to Sue. I feel too bad. I want

you to tell her that I left. Tell the kids that I love them and that I'll be in touch as soon as I get settled."

11

CRACKED - UP

Crack. A very descriptive name. Try it and soon you will crack. People under its addictive power will place everything else beneath its satanic feet.

Sex.
Money.
Integrity.
Relationships.

Ever wonder why the fight against drugs is so overwhelming? A powerful, sadistic enemy fuels the dark war. Crack cocaine grabs hold of everyone who experiences its seductive, destructive high.

This adversary lurked in the shadows of the seamy world I returned to when I fled Alaska in the spring of 1984. I headed for my sister's home in Anaheim, but took a month to reach my destination. Partying (really self-destructing) my way down the coast, I detoured to Reno for a reunion with the craps tables.

I finally called Sue from L.A. Her response was unbelievably forgiving: "I understand how you could have gotten involved with your ex-wife. I'll join you as soon as I can."

A couple weeks later she flew south, but how she ever endured the next several years can only be explained by the grace of God.

As for myself, I experienced deep anguish, shame, and guilt. It appeared that I cared for nothing except my own escapist pleasures, yet the seed of faith remained alive in my heart. God would break me somehow and accomplish the work that needed to be done. At the moment, I had burned all my bridges in Alaska. While no official judgment would be pronounced, I knew my latest failure had whipped up a storm of understandable negative reaction.

It looked like another graduate course in the School of Hard Knocks. Like the children of Israel, I would have to wander through the wilderness, learning the lessons God had tried to teach me through easier circumstances.

Despite my never-ending blunders, I vowed not to quit. Nevertheless, I planned to "drop out" for a while to cope while feeding myself with drugs and alcohol. Cowardly? I suppose so, but the nature of my sin dumped a heavy weight on my shoulders. After another miserable collapse, I felt like a spiritual pioneer trying to cross the Rocky Mountains in a three-wheeled wagon.

Insane Existence

In California, I pursued an insane lifestyle. Five times a week I drove to the golf course, grabbed a six pack of beer and headed for the greens. Other than nodding to a few regulars and getting high with a couple of guys, I avoided social contact. The fewer people who knew the truth about me, the better. After five or six hours of golf, I drove home, smoked some marijuana, ate a big dinner and then drove another hour to Gardena.

That city has legalized gambling, although poker is its only form. The lack of black jack or dice games, didn't bother me. I was addicted to gambling. I wasted hours at the card tables, some of my "stake" derived from small-time thievery that fueled my habits without draining away all of Sue's income.

In reflection, I marvel at the many states striving to become gambling havens. Casinos are a plague to be avoided. Their legalized existence teaches people that luck, rather than hard work, is the key to success.

My invitation to crack came through a card dealer. Smiling, he said, "I think you'll like it."

We started at eight o'clock and quickly used up our supply. Since dealers combed the streets in search of customers, obtaining more proved to be simple. By six the next morning, the drug and my $400 in cash had vanished. The high didn't seem so great compared with the expense. At least, that's what I thought.

The second time hooked me. Drug users love to pick apart the warning that you're addicted after one use. Whether it's two, three, or four times, the danger is real. The high is instantaneous and so powerful that people spend everything they have, do anything they must, to get more. Most prostitutes today aren't in the trade for the money, but the crack or some other drug. Give it to them and they'll oblige.

I wasted thousands of dollars on it, but I'll never know how much because of the blackouts that struck with increasing frequency. I would binge on heroin and liquor, and my life became a daily blur.

Meanwhile, Sue would come home from work and worry. Would I make it home that night? Would the police arrest me for intoxicated driving? Or would an official-sounding voice call during the wee hours to say, "Your husband's been killed in a wreck?"

Sometimes she would hunt me up in the card rooms. She didn't want me there; she hated the idea of her man of God mired in a pit of sin. Yet she came, waiting patiently in the lounge while I gambled on...and on...and on.

After a few months living with my sister, we moved in with a Christian couple near San Clemente. Thank God they went to church and took Sue with them!

One Sunday, Sue learned that evangelist James Robison would be speaking at Melodyland and invited me to attend. Since I had never heard him in person, I thought, "Why not?" However, near the end of his sermon that evening I got bored and stepped outside for a cigarette. Afterwards, I stood at the back of the auditorium, where Sue joined me as we waited for the friends who had driven us there.

Suddenly a funny look crossed her face, but before I could ask what was wrong, she said, "Joseph Woods and his wife, June, are coming up the aisle."

A year had passed since I ran from Anchorage, and during that time no communication had passed between us. The idea of confronting him made me nervous, but as I turned to greet them amazingly a quiet peace settled over me.

I offered my hand and they surprised us by inviting us to join them for Chinese food. Over a leisurely dinner, I confessed the truth about my backslid condition. "But," I added, "I'm not ready to get right with God, which is why I ran away. That's why I never wrote a letter of apology, because there's no need to do that until I'm ready to repent. I'm not ready and that's where it's at, Joe. I respect you and appreciate everything you've done, but I'm in a very dark time in my life."

Their encouragement and support left me thankful for their many years of friendship. They understood that things weren't easy, that I was behind in the battle, and yet they were able to minister love and hope. As I mentioned earlier, never underestimate the help you give a struggling saint. Joseph gave me a big hug and then quietly placed two twenty dollar bills in my hand. He and June said they loved us and would trust God for our restoration.

When the truth of my addictions threatened to surface in San Clemente, we packed up and moved an hour away to Escondido. There we stayed with an old friend from Alaska, a former student evangelist who had backslid. However, he was attending church and his life looked better than mine. I hoped he might provide an example of strength.

Capable in real estate and investments, he had struck it rich in the lucrative Alaska market. He owned a huge house, horses, and drove a Rolls Royce, when he wasn't tooling around in his Mercedes. He would take me out for $100 rounds of golf at posh courses and casually pick up the tab.

However, he had a drinking problem which he failed to recognize. Since I also refused to admit I had one, we fed off each other's craziness. One day as we talked about college football, I said, "The odds on this game in Las Vegas must be pretty good."

"What do you mean?"

"Well, they have odds in Vegas where you gamble."

"They gamble on football games in Vegas? We'd better go."

We hopped a jet there and he put up the money while I picked the teams. The first time he bet $30,000 and netted $10,000, handing me $1,000 as a commission.

The next weekend we flew back, but this time he lost $10,000 on $30,000 in bets. Coupled with a recent disaster in the commodities market, he dropped $150,000. The setbacks didn't dull his appetite. I wound up going back to Vegas, but a few weeks of the unreal atmosphere led to depression and discouragement. Perhaps the prayers of Sue and my friend's wife were thwarting the powers of darkness, removing joy from our sin.

I left Las Vegas and returned to my sister's in California, where Sue rejoined me. There we received an unexpected phone call from a Christian friend in Seattle who had backslid and now made his living in the cocaine trade. He invited us to fly up at Thanksgiving and spend a month with him. At first, we struck up a good friendship, sharing the drug while we talked about God. Even in our numbed state we could feel conviction, yet our bondage kept us trapped.

Sue and I didn't stay long, though, due to his unpredictable, drug-induced mood swings.

Thanks to friends who bought us a $300 car and another man who let us sleep on his living room floor, we managed to survive. This ugly turn of events weighed heavy on my fragile state of mind, and it didn't take long to choose to run again. This time, I left Sue so broke she had to move into a woman's boarding house.

I drove our beat-up car down the coast, stealing items that I could quickly convert to cash until I made it to Los Angeles. But the glitter of sin had no staying power. In a matter of weeks I tired of life there and impulsively set out for Miami, Florida, where I hoped for a new start. Instead I shook hands with the same old decadence.

"Another" Life-Changing Trip

On a trip up the East Coast, my life took its

fateful turn. I checked into a hotel in Charlotte, North Carolina, where I planned to relax and shoot some heroin I had bought on the streets.

As I lay there in that hotel room in Charlotte, floating through a heroin-fogged state, I turned on the TV. It "happened" to be tuned to the Charlotte-based PTL network. The Bakkers were talking about their program called the Opportunity Farm. Located on the grounds of Heritage USA, the ministry offered free room and board and an opportunity to get your head together. To someone living by the daily fruits of criminal-stained labors, free room and board sounded wonderful. But more importantly, PTL offered me the opportunity to escape the drug chains that had me so bound I might as well have been lashed to a set of tracks as a freight train chugged around the bend.

No matter how crazy my own experience sounds, there is an army of wandering souls traveling the same road. After mingling with many of them, I recognized common elements in our backgrounds. They were victims of sexual or physical abuse, divorce, bad childhoods - people unable to cope with unhappy lives or disappointments with parents or children. Many of these women have been molested, raped, or abused and have turned to prostitution, living only for the drugs that take their minds off reality. Many of the men were also sexually molested as youngsters and have been in and out of jail so many times "failure" is stamped on their brain. Some are capable of making a respectable living, but lacking any incentives, they shrug their shoulders and give in to the world's sick alternatives.

Life is no picnic on this misty, gray street of despair. I chose not only a disgusting existence, but a dangerous one. One street person's moral code might be, "I would smack a guy over the head, but I would never shoot him with a shotgun," while the next brags, "I would shoot a guy with a shotgun, but never a woman." A third doesn't care what harm he inflicts, as long as you have something he wants.

Although this way of life surrounds us, it's not so easy to see. Unless "good" folks happen to confront the miserable, they don't often think about them. If they do, they often shrug, "Well, they're choosing to live this way and they deserve it for living such sinful lives."

Don't misunderstand me. I'm not blaming anyone for my choices. I reaped what I sowed. The consequences matched the depth of my sin. However, those who embrace the "little" sins, like gossip, bitterness, gluttony, and judgmentalism, ultimately pay the price, too. Their lives become symbolized by lukewarm, compromising Christianity that never reaches out but pretends to have great power.

It doesn't take superhuman feats of strength to go out and seek those who are hurting. You can't put a noose around their neck and yank them back into church. But you can try again instead of simply giving up when someone ignores your outstretched hand.

Because a host of people extended themselves and never gave up on me, I am alive today. That includes one couple who served as the object of public scorn, mocking, and ridicule: Jim and the former Mrs. Tammy Bakker.

Twelve years earlier I traveled with Joseph Woods to Charlotte as he was invited to be interviewed on the Jim Bakker Show. I was introduced on the TV program as a young pastor getting ready to start a new church in Atlanta, Georgia. Now I was back as a disgraced fallen leader. But, I was welcomed and accepted into their program of restoration for broken people.

12

Into Treatment

Christian Disneyland.

The dazzling water park, theme park, swimming pools, private mall - after life in the dirty fast lane, *Hertitage USA* looked like heaven. The eight men from the Opportunity Farm would walk around the grounds with a sense of awe.

My decision to go there thrilled Sue, who lost touch with me after I left L.A. A PTL fan, when I called her from the treatment center, she excitedly quit her job and moved to Charlotte. After finding a job, she visited me several times a week. Her support proved invaluable during my three-month stay, since more than once my strength wavered.

We attended Bible classes half a day and spent the other half helping out with the dozens of continuing work projects. I worked in the mailroom, out in the bean fields, on painting projects, and other miscellaneous endeavors.

I'm very grateful the program was there when I needed it. Despite the events that led to his prison term, Jim Bakker worked to bring countless numbers of people to Christianity and many Godly blessings. PTL gave away millions of dollars to the poor and operated all kinds of legitimate programs that helped many thousands of people.

The Opportunity Farm, which later became known as Fort Hope, enabled me to remain sober for three consecutive months. Before that, I struggled to stay straight for more than three days. Besides Bible study and work projects, once a week they divided us into small support groups and encouraged us to talk about the predicament that led us there.

Unfortunately, I had a run-in with one of the chief counselors. A believer in the extreme position of demon possession doctrines — he thought demons possessed nearly everyone, including Christians — he constantly tried to tell me they were my problem. I argued, "No, it's a flesh problem. It's learning how to come to grips with the pain and responsibilitys of life." He also said things like, "If you smoke cigarettes, you're going to hell," to which I responded, "How does the saved by grace, not by works doctrine fit into your theology?" Similar conflicts continually kept us at odds. However, I left with a positive attitude towards the program, realizing those doctrinal clashes represented a conflict with one person.

Weekend Warrior

One truth that eluded me during my stay at PTL was my alcoholism. I continued to deny its existence, insisting that I had mastery over this *little weakness*. The silliness of that notion can be seen through the daily bottle habit I developed within a few weeks. Yes, I backslid again.

Because of our meager finances, Sue and I checked into a cheap hotel in downtown Charlotte, where a lot of drug users lived. That type of surroundings were second nature to me, though it took courage for Sue to live there. What scared me were the money pressures caused by my wild living; given my alcoholic ways, it didn't take much stress for my defense systems to crumble.

Sue was busy at the office one Friday when I called and left a message that I had gone to Atlantic City and would be back on Monday. Through my streetwise ways, I had saved up a bankroll for a quick weekend escape.

Why return to the gutter? There are no easy answers, except to say that I had no strong commitments or vision to keep my life on an even keel. Even my relationship with Sue, who stuck by me longer than anyone else would have, didn't motivate me. Lacking a clear direction, I fell into old habits with the same ease I used in uncorking a bottle of cheap wine.

In Atlantic City, I checked into a hotel and hit the gaming tables, where a losing streak quickly thinned my bankroll.

"Well, if I'm going to lose my money anyway, I might as well get stoned before I lose it all," I shrugged.

Outside, I easily found cocaine, heroin, and two prostitutes to share it with. We spent the whole night driving around town, sharing the same needle. In the modern AIDS era, you would have sworn I had a death wish.

At sunup, I told one of the women it was time to leave, but correctly suspecting the other lady and I had stashed some drugs somewhere, she refused. After a futile argument, I jumped out of the car, opened one door and dragged her onto the sidewalk, kicking and screaming. A bystander called the cops.

After settling us down, they ran my name through their computer. Since there were no outstanding warrants for my arrest, they told me I was free to go.

"The only problem is your license plates expired three months ago," said one of the officers. "We can't let you drive the car until you take care of that. So you'll have to walk."

"Well, how am I going to get back to North Carolina?"

"That's your problem."

Not only was I without a car, the last of my money had disappeared up my veins. Later in the day, as I hitchhiked out of town, I started sweating and vomiting from heroin withdrawal. After spending the night in a Rescue Mission, I thumbed a ride to Philadelphia and called Traveler's Aid for help. They contacted Sue to ask if she would reimburse them, but she refused.

Thanks to all the grief I put her through and some friendly advice from her boss, she finally understood that constantly bailing me out of troubles only enabled me to get into more.

I called her the next day and she again refused.

"I understand," I said — and I did. "You've endured a lot. I'll make it back my own way."

That night, I stayed in a Hare Krishna mission, where I walked in the prodigal son's shoes. In the middle of the night, as I went to close a window to shield my head from rain dripping on me, I stepped on a dirty nail. Blood gushed through the torn skin. I shrugged, wrapped a sock around it, and went back to sleep.

I then moved to a Christian mission and earned twenty dollars on a painting job. I also convinced a woman from a Presbyterian church to give me the cash to purchase a bus ticket to the town where my father lived. I hoped to find enough temporary work while staying there to pay for transportation to Charlotte.

I had nothing left to take to a pawn shop for some quick cash. Like most drug addicts I had already hocked my wedding ring, and my wife's wedding ring. Years earlier I surprised Sue with an expensive gold nugget Bulova watch for her birthday. During one of my binges I asked her for the watch so I could have money to gamble, drink and do more drugs.

Sue never had much and the little she had I took to feed my habit. Amazingly she always forgave me and seldom complained about the insensitive, selfish, cruel and unusual anguish I put her through. Did I feel bad about it? Yes! Yet I continued to put her through mental and emotional torture, as I continued down my road of self-destruction.

Sickness, which began setting in at the mission, worsened when I arrived at Dad's house. I tried looking for work, but found none. By the time I dragged myself in, fatigue wracked my body. I fell asleep on the couch, and because of my past problems my latest stepmother thought this "sickness" was a fake. Fearing I wanted to move in, she demanded I leave.

"Son, I'm sorry, but you've got to go," Dad said when he broke the news. "I'll buy your bus ticket to Charlotte."

Treatment Center #2

I spent the first two weeks back in Charlotte still sick in bed, which is how I saw the daytime promotional spot for a CBS television special on AIDS. When Sue came home from work, I told her about it and she asked why I wanted to watch it.

"Oh, I just think it'll be interesting," I lied, fearing that the progressive sickness and leg sores that had shown up in Philly were the early signs. The show reviewed those very symptoms, confirming my suspicions. Lying there, I struggled to accept the inevitability of death. My thoughts changed from the usual concerns about bills, tomorrow's plans, and the future. If death awaited me, what mattered was how I spent my remaining time on earth. Honoring my family and God, and doing something of a positive nature before I departed suddenly became my overwhelming desire. I had no concern about whether I would go to heaven. I had been saved and knew that would be my final destination. I actually looked forward to it. Accepting death gave me a new motivation to be productive.

Finally I turned to Sue: "I am pretty well convinced I have AIDS."

Bursting into tears, she sobbed, "I don't want to die."

"Well, you're going to heaven, so what does it matter? Everything will be better."

"I'm not ready to die," she protested. "I want to hang out for awhile."

"Well, we're going to have to deal with it and make the best of it," I said, laying back against my pillow as I gasped for breath. "You'd better take me to the hospital."

X-rays showed that I had pneumonia, yet I didn't want to get checked for AIDS. I may have adjusted to the idea of facing death, but not enough to hear a doctor say that a terminal illness ran through my blood.

However, after my latest escapade I knew I needed help. Since Sue's construction employer was about to send her to Virginia for eight months, it made sense to return to treatment. I had already found a Christian program called *"Rebound."*

An interdenominational center, their free, open-door policy meant my lack of finances didn't matter. Nor did the fact I had only been out of PTL for a couple months. When they asked, "Do you want to get your life together?" I enthusiastically answered, "Yes."

After checking in, I discovered I didn't have AIDS. I donated blood for some quick cash, and passed the standard screening test they ran. Equally important during my first week was the mandatory Alcoholics Anonymous meeting.

"Hi, My Name Is Michael. I'm an Alcoholic"

I harbored a negative attitude towards AA, even though my prior exposure consisted of only one meeting. But that evening a 38-year-old actress described her behavior patterns that demonstrated severe problems. She confessed about her never-ending string of denials. I marveled at how closely her symptoms matched mine. Finally, the revelation hit me between the eyes. Finally, I came out of my denial about my alcoholism.

When she finished, I confessed that I, too, was an alcoholic and I received my first coin, stamped with AA and "One Day At A Time." Sometimes people laugh at program "trinkets," yet the coin is an effective symbol of the goal alcoholics strive for each day.

After the meeting, I called Sue.

"Guess what? I greeted her. I'm an alcoholic."

"What are you talking about?" she responded in worried tones. "Are you still at Rebound?"

"Yeah, I'm still here. I went to an AA meeting tonight and this woman talked and I related to everything she said. She's a alcoholic and I'm an alcoholic. I've got problems and I need help, but I'm going to deal with it."

Damaged Goods

You could say I was a "drugaholic," too. Both are compulsive, addictive behaviors. Since alcohol is legal and socially respectable, it doesn't carry the stigma of illegal substances, yet its long-term effects are more damaging. At Rebound I first learned about the harm alcohol does to the brain and liver and how it actually breaks down the body.

Most Christians define alcoholism as strictly a moral problem while AA labels it a disease over which people have no control. I believe it's both. There's no denying the moral failings of reaching for the bottle, regardless of the reasons for it. However, evidence about alcoholics' hereditary disposition and weakness towards it has been uncovered. And with prolonged use, it becomes a disease. Millions of brain cells burn out, the liver is shot full of holes, and normal thought processes tilt off balance.

We also studied the Bible. Because of my previous teaching and preaching experience I faced the danger of smudginess, but tried to carefully guard against that attitude. I concentrated on listening, applying, and growing.

After three months, I felt I had learned all that I could at Rebound. Yet I recognized the depths of my weakness and decided to obtain a non-Christian perspective by entering a state-run treatment center. I chose a program near Black Mountain, in the hills of the northwestern part of North Carolina.

I spent a month there, but left a couple days early to trying to help a man I befriended at the center. He was a backslidden Baptist, twenty-six years old; I exhorted, and shared some thoughts about God... and later prayed with him as he rededicated his life to God.

A week later he told me that he had AIDS, which he believed he had contracted from one of eight different prostitutes he visited during a drunken separation from his wife and two children. He had swollen lymph nodes under his arms, a common sign, but I advised him to take a second test and tell his wife.

"I can't tell her," he shook his head. "She'll tell my dad and he'll disown me and it's over."

Nonetheless, he took another test. When it came back positive, the director kicked him out of the center. I didn't want him to go alone, so

I left with him and we drove to Charlotte. But on the outside, he quickly dropped out of the mainstream. Like many AIDS patients, he wanted to die alone because of the embarrassment and fear of judgment.

Back in Charlotte, I faced the challenge of leading a clean, sober life. Since nicotine is a drug, I couldn't even smoke a cigarette. Sue would be in Virginia for two more months, so I would have to find work, a place to live and keep it together - on my own. I had to meet this challenge if I hoped to convince my wife I had finally changed. I desperately wanted to succeed. By God's grace I continued my journey one day at a time.

13

THE ROCKY ROAD BACK

After six months of sobriety I relapsed again. I allowed the monkey out of the cage. The monster jumped on my back and wanted to run. More crack, heroin and spending nights with women who weren't my wife.

Why?

Alcoholics and other addicts seize any excuse, any setback, any interruption of their fragile routine, to return to familiar habits. The deceitfulness of sin blinds them before destroying them.

My sickness and disease was a direct result of my sin! It was a morality problem. My character was questionable and I was not to be trusted. The facts were that I had not humbled myself before God. Yes I made attempts, but I continued to hold on to the different forms of pride and self-sufficiency. My Heavenly Father chastened me because I needed it. He continues to chasten me because He loves me and I need it! God's grip of love was upon me.

Back to Seattle

Pastor James Smith knew I was sick. Yet amazingly he and the church leadership invited Sue and I back to Seattle to become part of their congregation. With such a loving offer of reconciliation, we had only to choose our moving date. I was willing, but very weak. I was afraid.

The church welcomed us with open arms. A couple weeks before we arrived, Smith had told the congregation about our arrival. "Part of the ministry of the church is to restore those who have fallen," he said. "Mike and Sue have gone through a lot. He has failed and needs help, so let's try to be sensitive and reach out to them with love and understanding."

My first relapse occurred on the job. Painting the interior of a house, I spotted a marijuana cigarette lying on the coffee table. I flirted with temptation for about an hour, walking by, staring at it and, mulling over the idea of smoking it. Finally, I gave in to the lust of my flesh.

I confessed this sin to the associate pastor and my wife, and managed to maintain sobriety for another six months. However, as my business grew to five employees, so did the pressures of meeting payroll and suppliers' bills and wondering whether I could collect from contractors to keep the ball rolling.

After my second relapse, which included more, alcohol, drugs, gambling, crime, and etc. two elders came to visit, encouraging me to read the Bible daily, pray and remain accountable to them. One of them was quite concerned about my relapse and said,

"God has already given you unprecedented grace."

I thought to myself "Is he suggesting that I'm the worst sinner that has ever lived?" Their hearts were right, but they were not able to effectively minister strength and hope into my spirit.

The next morning when an employee and fellow drug abuser who had borrowed my expensive ($3,000) spray rig didn't show up for a job, I imagined the worst. Quickly, I convinced myself that he had sold the rig to buy drugs, leaving me holding the bag.

The thought of severe financial pressure proved to be more than I could face. Telling Sue I was going to Los Angeles to pick up some belongings a friend had placed in storage for us, I quickly hit the road for Reno. There I stayed stoned and gambled away $1,200 in three days before continuing to California for another fling, smoking crack and gambling in the card rooms.

Six weeks after I left, I returned to Seattle and stopped at James Smith's house.

"Are you going to spend the rest of your life doing this?" he frowned when he opened the front door. "When are you going to straighten up?"

14
CHRISTIAN SUPPORT

Failures. They litter the landscape outside America's drug and alcohol treatment centers. While many administrators promise hurting people and their families a cure the fact is most of their patients relapse.

Who is to blame? Not the administrators or counselors who give of themselves in a sincere effort to help those in bondage. But we're up against a powerful enemy; as Ephesians 6:12 warns, *we wrestle not against human beings, but with evil principalities and the rulers of spiritual darkness.* The blood of Jesus and grace of God is America's only hope of winning its drug war.

In July of 1988 I went through my fourth — and I hope, last — treatment program. During my four-week stay, I gained a deeper appreciation for the common needs in the lives of hurting people, no matter how different their backgrounds. There were 130 patients in the program; I was the only ex-preacher there. My roommate was the 6' 5", 300-pound son of a prostitute. His father had been her pimp before he was murdered dealing drugs. Another man bore the scars of a dozen failures in similar treatment programs. But we were all human beings crying out for healing, understanding, love and consideration.

Our breakdowns are so extreme and frequent that most people quickly lose patience with us. However, unless you have endured the wars of temptation, struggle, and defeat against a powerful foe, you cannot fathom how hard many people strive to come to grips with their problem, only to fall.

While in the center, I thought seriously about developing an idea for a Christian support group that I had conceived in North Carolina, while I was at Rebound.

After several AA meetings there, I realized the program positively affected those who were serious about achieving sobriety. Yet I also saw that AA had certain limitations for a Christian. It could not meet the believer's greater needs because of its attitude regarding a generic "higher power." The group, the sky, the Great White Spirit, a light bulb - whatever name or god you selected was perfectly all right.

AA takes that position because it is the only way their group can be open to everyone. It's not my intention to knock AA, because God used AA to help me face my alcoholism. I believe God is using AA powerfully and many thousands are not only getting sober but they are also beginning to think about spirituality. I believe AA is a stepping stone that God can use to bring many to Christ, and also to bring the reality of alcoholism to Christians. There are many alcoholic Christians in denial. If the church doesn't help them, God will use AA, even though they don't claim to be a religious organization.

In North Carolina, I wrote down my basic vision: to set up a group that would be identified as a Christian support organization for backsliders. People with life-dominating problems, whether alcohol, drugs, sexual immorality, overeating, gossip, gambling, or other bad habits. In this setting, they could deal honestly with their problems.

Many Christians have not confronted this need, since many members deny that the problems even exist in their clean churches. Yet we have transvestites going to church and homosexuals speaking in tongues and then going out and secretively committing all kinds of bizarre sexual immorality. Wife-beaters, porno addicts, child molesters, habitual liars, obese food addicts, prescription drug addicts, marijuana addicts, and nicotine addicts hiding to smoke so that their testimony isn't damaged.

Every kind of sin imaginable is committed by those who bear the name "Christian." Many deceived, self-righteous pastors are quick to say "those kinds of people are not in my church."

Every church of average size has backsliders as members. Outside the Church is a legion of ex-members who have turned their backs on God to pursue a life of sin and self-fulfillment as they lick their wounds. They, too, need to be reached. Backsliders are everywhere!

You who are spiritual restore with meekness the brother who has fallen into sin. That's what the Bible teaches and that's what I and so many like me need.

Reaching Out To Backsliders

My vision consisted of reaching out, encouraging, and restoring backsliders to spiritual health and church fellowship. The Word is clear: we are not to ignore associating with other believers, because their support helps us to remain on a faithful walk with God. We must not forsake the assembling of ourselves together. We need each other!

While I don't agree with all of AA's practices, I like the way they conduct their meetings, with an opportunity for everyone to share their experience, strength, and hope. Aside from restrictions on swearing and smoking, I planned to run *Christians In Recovery* in a similar manner. Everyone would have a chance to talk about anything they wanted, including serious personal problems that are "taboo" in most church settings. At church the preacher talks and everyone else listens and there's a need for that format. But recovering Christians have a great need to talk also. They need to share their pain and victory, but, in most churches they never get a chance.

However, doctrinal debates would have no place in the group. It would be a place for individual and collective healing and positive fellowship. Backsliders are desperately in need of love because their misguided actions often result in self condemnation.

Besides forming friendships, people who come to meetings burdened with the self-image of "weirdo" or "pervert" would discover they weren't isolated cases. Finding that many others are in similar predicaments, some worse than their own, encourages and gives hope to these Christians in recovery. In coming out of isolation, these people would confess their sin, be lifted up in prayer, and cultivate some hope from the dust of their desert experience.

As God provided the resources, I envisioned

groups springing up across the United States. Eventually, I hoped Christians In Recovery would grow to include a Christian treatment facility. Combined with that would be a rural Retreat Center where church leaders who have fallen could spend a month in an atmosphere of love and understanding, with no judgment or pressure. Therapy would be offered so pastors could honestly discuss life-changing issues. None of this has happened yet, but it hasn't changed my desire to see it come to pass.

However, when I emerged from the treatment center in Seattle, in 1988 I didn't automatically decide to proceed. I just knew I had to do something productive. As a God-ordained minister, I had to serve in some type of ministry. Yet I knew I wouldn't be re-ordained for a long time; my behavior had disqualified me from any position of church leadership. "There must be something I can do that's legitimate," I thought. "Something that God will approve of, that is biblical. Helping backsliders...there's nothing wrong with that. You don't have to be ordained or be an elder. All you need is a heart and a desire to help others." I knew I was qualified to do that. One sinner trying to help another sinner.

Because of my history, the church would have preferred I wait a year. But I knew because of my past patterns that I might not make it through another year. My survival depended on doing something to reach out and help others, in turn receiving help from them. Strengthening and being strengthened.

"Jim, I've decided that I need to do something," I told Smith after reviewing my earlier outline and writing down some additional plans. "I feel God leading me to start an organization called Backsliders Anonymous (later changed to Christian's In Recovery).

I also began formulating a ten-step program, somewhat like AA's well-known twelve-step program but a Christian-based set of guidelines (see chapter fifteen.) I then visited an attorney to incorporate the group in the state of Washington so that when the church gave its official blessing, I would be prepared.

Like most groups, this one began very slowly. The first meeting consisted of some informal discussions with a man who had also just been released from the treatment center. He was staying in our home while readjusting to society. We read the ten steps, had open discussion and prayed.

"Well, what's happening with me is I'm learning to handle life one day at a time," I led off the discussion. "I've been going out to lunch with different people for fellowship and that's been very encouraging. I'm reading the Word. I'm trying not to worry about money or the future because I have to take care of today until I get established. I'm trying to make this transition slowly. If I don't know what throws me off, then it can be easy to fall back into the same trap."

Sam shared his fears and concerns, particularly about his separation from his wife. She had grown tired of the drug-soaked ways of a man whose habit helped cut short a promising college basketball career and, fifteen years later, threatened to destroy his life. He confessed about the loneliness that dogged him.

We encouraged each other and agreed that we needed to establish a track record of sobriety. I wish I could say Sam turned into a rousing success story after that first meeting. He had prayed to receive salvation the first week he lived with us, but severely relapsed when he collected his first paycheck. I allowed him to borrow our car to go to the bank and he disappeared for three days. When he returned, my camera had disappeared from the glove compartment and the interior was partially damaged from his frantic search for crack. He mistakenly believed I had hidden some in the car during one of my earlier escapades.

When he finally appeared, he walked up with

his head hung low and said, "I guess I gotta go now, huh?"

Studying his guilty, sagging frame for a moment, I knew just how he felt. I could hardly be mad at someone whose actions mirrored my own, so I tried to be loving but firm in my response.

"Well, it's like this. You've got to go if you're not serious about following God," I said. "But if you're serious about following God and you want God to forgive you, He will forgive you. If He forgives you, that means that you've got another chance. So if you want to continue with Jesus, I'll give you another chance."

The Group Expands

The next meeting included Shawn, an old friend and fellow backslider. When I invited him and his wife over for dinner, I didn't know our church had excommunicated him for continuous drinking and neglect of his wife. For months, they patiently tried to counsel with him, but finally gave up.

He talked that night about his hurt and a profound need for fellowship. Despite the realization his actions had created the mess, flames of resentment still flickered in his chest for the way the church had reacted towards him. He talked of the need for healing from bitterness, plus support while he worked his way through that and other problems.

Shawn was on his way home later that night when he pulled up to a stop sign, yanked a pack of cigarettes out of his pocket and crumpled them into a brown-stained heap of paper.

"Honey, I've suffered enough," he said to his wife. "I'm giving my life back to God."

As I write this, he has been clean and sober for over two years. From that night on, he faithfully attended the original Backsliders Anonymous chapter in Seattle and organized a group in his own church. He and his wife opened their large home to other backsliders, seeking to restore them to a clean and sober lifestyle.

We had a few more meetings in my home before expanding our agenda by inviting guest speakers. I called on some friends who had also fought their way back to describe how the Lord had enabled them to straighten out their messed-up lives.

Do you remember the cocaine dealer whose paranoia and crude treatment caused us to move out of his home not long after one of our return trips to Seattle? Rick was our first speaker. The story of how he broke out of his drug chains, leaving behind a "business" that generated more than $100,000 a month, proved particularly powerful.

Tim came next. A personable musician and evangelist, he had trained with Youth With A Mission and ministered in Hawaii, leading many souls to Christ. But gradually he backslid into drugs and the rock-and-roll world. His face lit up as he described how the Lord welcomed him back with as much warmth as the first Prodigal Son.

At that point the meetings outgrew our home. In early 1989 we began using space offered at a church by a pastor.

The first speaker in our new quarters was a member of the Seattle affiliate of a national ministry to homosexuals. He discussed the burden he felt for reaching those trapped in the gay lifestyle, which includes many closeted in Christian circles. He told of attending church for years while secretly living in homosexual perversion, until he finally faced the problem, confessed it, repented and found forgiveness and deliverance.

"How can you be a homosexual and go to church?" you might ask. But how can you be a glutton and a disciple? How can you be an alcoholic and attend church? How could Jimmy Swaggart preach so hard against perversion when he was practicing acts of perversion for years? How can you commit any sin and consider yourself a Christian? All of us need help breaking down the barriers that separate us from the Lord, no matter what our particular area of sin might be.

To expand our outreach, we scraped together donations to establish a $400-a-month budget for radio spots, sixty-second testimonials that called attention to our meetings. I also appeared on a talk show on the station that aired our advertisements, and established a twenty-four-hour hotline, a separate phone that rang into the ministry's office — our spare bedroom. We also published our first newsletter, giving the group more credibility and helping spread the word about our meetings.

These steps helped boost attendance over several months from six to eight people to ten, then fifteen, twenty, and upward until we reached forty.

Six months after he started coming to our meetings, a member of an Assembly of God church who had a drinking problem decided it was time to use our principles to establish a chapter in his own church. Then came Ferndale, Washington Chicago and Bladensburg, Ohio another in Seattle, then Charlotte, North Carolina...and eventually, I pray, in all fifty states.

There are many alcohol and drug support groups operating today under many names, but most of them have a distinguishing characteristic. The mention of Jesus Christ in their meetings is infrequent and uncomfortable. It's not the accepted format, and while such groups have every right to conduct their meetings in whatever manner they choose, struggling Christians need to be able to discuss their faith or lack of faith. *Christians In Recovery* gears meetings to helping in Christian ways - by offering prayer, understanding, and healing in the name of Christ.

This is why I would love to see all churches open their doors to this type of ministry. By their very nature, most churches cannot meet all the needs of backsliders and people in recovery. Pastors have an obligation to shepherd the flock, beginning with preaching and teaching the Word of God. They also have the accompanying duties of visitation, prayer, funerals and weddings that create additional time demands.

Christians In Recovery. They're a unique group, with a need for healing and restoration. *Hurting people getting help — by helping hurting people.*

The Backslider

By Michael Premo

I was a loser, temporarily insane
Escaped from reality, shot herion in my veins.

Alcohol and drugs will sooth my pain
LSD and sniffing glue done fried my brain.

Addicted to gambling, stealing to survive
My family went hungry, my mother died.

A diabolical delusion of confusion
The Devil wants me dead!

Jesus loves me this I know
My grandmother told me, a long time ago.

God, I'm a sinner
My hands are unclean.

Forgive me and cleanse me
Remove darkness and shame.

Renew my mind, restore my soul
I'm a backslider, I want to come home.

Amazing grace how sweet the sound
I once was lost but now I'm found.

I now it's real, I know it's true
God, I love you!

15

Backsliders Everywhere!

"My brothers, if one of you should wander from the truth and someone should bring him back, remember this: Whosoever turns a sinner from the error of his way will save him from death and cover over a multitude of sins." *James 5:19-20*

Backsliding

If you don't think it's a common problem, consider this: whenever I visit jails or other institutions I ask, "How many of you have been genuinely born again and then backslid?" At least eighty percent of the audience raise their hands. As a guest speaker in churches, when I ask, "How many have backslid at some point in their lives?" seventy-five percent respond.

Many church members would be shocked to see what lies under the false veil of many Christians. Don't blame the church, though people instinctively conceal their sin. It's an ingrained human trait. It originated in the Garden of Eden when Adam and Eve tried to hide their sin from God by shifting the blame for their disobedience on someone else. That tendency has been with us ever since. (Have you ever known anyone who didn't try to put their own actions in the most favorable light possible?)

Nor should we be surprised that church members have problems. The struggle with our flesh — the lust of the flesh, the lust of the eyes and the pride of life spelled out in 1 John 2:16 — is normal. We don't easily conquer it, nor can we ever assume that we aren't subject to falling. (If you doubt that statement, check the latter part of Galatians 6:1.) *Be careful when you think you stand, lest you fall.*

There are times when Christians are easily deceived into thinking that they are something that they are not. Pride comes before the fall. Tempted by Satan, people become fooled into believing their fleshly righteousness makes them better than less mature believers. They elevate themselves and think that they are able to judge others. Before they realize it, they become modern Pharisees, hypocrites whose religiosity ruins their spiritual effectiveness. Pious and pompous, they can't minister to sinners and real people. "Churchianity" blinds them.

Such self-righteousness creates the type of

Christian who puts up the good front, wears the proper smile, uses the spiritual vocabulary and acts like his or her life is all together. Such folks are quick to condemn and judge. When this attitude prevails, it prevents the creation of an atmosphere of grace, mercy, and restoration in the church. Legalism and self-righteous Christians impart death and will kill the growth of any local church.

Members have to be constantly reminded that they are still sinners. Just as we were originally saved by grace, so too we are saved daily by grace. We are in need of continuous forgiveness. As long as we are mindful of our sinful condition, then we'll be ever slow to point fingers at someone who, in reality, is just like us.

Creating a gentle, grace-filled atmosphere in our churches is of critical importance. Otherwise, backsliders who visit will sense judgment and self-righteousness and leave, sometimes never to return to any congregation. However, if a church walks in a forgiving spirit, then backsliders who are paranoid, afraid of how they will be received, will feel comfortable. They will attain a sense of security as they realize, "These people are just like me. They understand. They're not going to reject or abuse me, but accept, love, and encourage me."

By living in and tasting of the dark world that surrounds us, I can testify that there are probably more backsliders outside of the church than Christians in the pews. If we can tap into the lives of these people and see a move of holiness and love sweep across our congregations, then the Church will experience true revival.

Through my unpleasant experiences, I sensed the need for the church to be more aggressive and diligent in reaching out to struggling Christians. Dealing with backsliders is not easy. It's very time-consuming and has the potential for incredible frustration. However, it's also very rewarding to see someone who has battled severe problems finally root their lives in God's Word and fulfill their destiny and purpose in God's plan.

Often churches have the attitude that if a person backslides and leaves, "They will just have to learn things the hard way." The hard way means they will have to do it all on their own. But what they need is help: from the pastor, the elders, deacons, and the brothers and sisters. Backsliders need Christians who will go out of their way to reach out and confirm their love and concern.

Millions of church goers have memorized hundreds of scriptures, attended all kinds of spiritual seminars, read all kinds of books by the experts and are well on their way to becoming theological experts. Yet they don't have a burden to get in their car, drive down the road, and knock on a backslider's door to offer love and assistance. The good shepherd will leave the ninety-nine and go after that one sheep who has gone astray. Love will compel us to go after those in need.

Knowledge is important, as is studying and memorizing scripture. However, just as we must be hearers of the Word, we must be doers of the Word.

In the book of Revelation, Jesus tells the church of Laodicea that because they are neither hot nor cold, but lukewarm, He will spew them out of His mouth. Earlier, He also warns the church at Ephesus to repent and do the things it did when first saved. Do we remember our enthusiasm in the early days of our salvation? Were we excited? Eager to help others? As we grow in the Lord, there is a danger of becoming lukewarm...even cold. But as revival comes in our lives, we will want to help each other, including the backslidden brothers and sisters. Honesty will prevail in our churches, instead of religious put-ons.

1 John 1:9 says, *"If we confess our sins, He is faithful and just and will forgive us our sins and purify us from all unrighteousness."*

The Word also tells us in James 5:16 to confess our faults to each other that we might be healed.

At Christians In Recovery, we place a premium on honesty. The first step in dealing with problems such as alcohol, drugs, gambling, or overeating is to admit there is a problem. Then God can begin to heal and restore the person.

Next, backsliders must break out of their mold of isolation and seek relationships with people they can trust. The people who attend our meetings have experienced pain, suffering, and the shame of brokenness and failure. Because they have faltered so many times themselves, they are slow to judge. This non-critical attitude helps to foster vital encouragement, strength, and support.

The third thing we do is direct people into a Christian church of their choosing, one where they can develop a relationship with the leadership. They need a good pastor or mature lay member to take them under his wing, shepherd them, and ground them in the Word of God. As they learn more about the Bible and church life, they can root out negative attitudes that they might have towards the church. It is mandatory to have a healthy attitude toward the local Church. No matter what its shortcomings are, the Church deserves our respect and support. Every Christian needs a local church where they are appreciated, loved and encouraged to minister in some capacity according to their gifts and abilities.

We open our meetings with prayer, followed by a reading of our Ten Steps For Restoration. After that, we go around the table and everyone has an opportunity to talk about issues in their lives. We don't force them to speak, but we strongly encourage them to share their heart.

Breaking down the silent barriers is a key to healing for those in recovery. Because of all the turmoil, stress, anxiety, and hardships they have faced. *Confession is good for the soul!*

Often Christians will backslide because of pride or immaturity. Without a Biblical foundation, these two areas pose major stumbling blocks.

So we try to work on them. If a person has an exalted self-opinion, he or she will be quickly humbled at our meetings; we will let them know, in love, that pride, foolishness, or playing head games has no place in a Christians In Recovery meeting.

Since we don't have Bible studies at our meetings, we can't fully develop someone's scriptural maturity, but through encouraging them to rejoin a church, we hope to achieve that goal for each member.

Christians In Recovery Prayer

Have mercy on me, O God,
according to your unfailing love;
according to your great compassion
blot out my transgressions.
Wash away all my iniquity and cleanse me from my sin.
For I know my transgressions,
and my sin is always before me.
Against you, you only, have I sinned
and done what is evil in your sight,
so that you are proved right when you speak
and justified when you judge.
Surely you desire truth in the inner parts;
you teach wisdom in the inmost place.
Cleanse me with hyssop, and I will be clean;
wash me, and I will be whiter than snow.
Let me hear joy and gladness;
let the bones you have crushed rejoice.
Hide your face from my sins and blot out all my iniquity.
Create in me a pure heart, O God,
and renew a steadfast spirit within me.
Do not cast me from your presence
or take your Holy Spirit from me.
Restore to me the joy of your salvation
and grant me a willing spirit, to sustain me.
Then I will teach transgressors your ways
and sinners will turn back to you.

Psalm 51:1-13

Christians In Recovery
Steps For Restoration

1. Admitted we were a backslider with negative life controlling habits, that our lives were empty and unfulfilled.

2 Cor. 1:9 We felt we were doomed to die and saw how powerless we were to help ourselves: but that was good, for then we put everything into the hands of God, who alone could save us, for he can even raise the dead.

2. Came to believe that only by the grace of God could we be restored to soundness of mind and spiritual health.

Psalm 30:2,3 O Lord my God, I pleaded with you, and you gave me my health again. You brought me back from the brink of the grave, from death itself, and here I am alive.

3. Made a searching and fearless moral inventory of ourselves.

Lamentations 3:40 Let us search and try our ways, and turn again to the Lord.

4. Admitted to God, and another person, the exact nature of our sin.

James 5:16 Therefore, confess your sins to one another, and pray for one another, so that you may be healed.

5. Made a decision to turn our will over to God and daily follow the teachings of the Bible.

Isaiah 26:3 He will keep in perfect peace all those who trust in him, whose thoughts turn often to the Lord! Trust in the Lord always, for in the Lord Jehovah is your everlasting strength."

6. Understanding the need for encouragement to grow towards love and good deeds, we united ourselves with Christ's church.

Hebrews 10:25 Not forsaking our own assembling together, as is the habit of some, but encouraging one another; and all the more, as you see the day drawing near.

7. Humbly asked God to give us grace and courage to follow the example of Jesus Christ the Lord and Savior.

James 4:10 Humble yourselves in the sight of the Lord, and he shall lift you up.

8. Made a list of all persons we had offended, and became willing to make amends whenever possible except when to do so would injure them or others.

Matt. 5:23,24 If therefore you are presenting your offering at the altar, and there remember that your brother has something against you, leave your offering there before the altar, and go your way; first be reconciled to your brother, and then come and present your offering.

9. Sought through prayer, study of His Word, and meditation, to daily keep close fellowship with God.

James 4:8 Draw near to God and He will draw near to you.

10. Having a spiritual revival as a result of God's grace, we will endeavor, with humility, to share the message of God's love and forgiveness to other backsliders.

Eph. 2:10 It is God himself who has made us what we are and given us new lives from Christ Jesus: and long ages ago he planned that we should spend these lives in helping others.

The testimony of a restored backslider can be a tremendous asset to any church (after the person has proven himself and the congregation is comfortable that he has achieved some stability.) As the Word says, those who are forgiven much also love much.

Naturally, backsliders must keep their end of this bargain. They have to learn to follow through on their commitments, join the church, faithfully attend, get grounded in the Word and repent (turn from sinful behavior). They must set their attitude away from the material and the worldly and pursue the spiritual blessings of God.

Satan is real. Millions of his demons are alive and filled with hate, spreading their confusion and insanity to anyone they can reach. You can see that by attending one of our meetings and hearing dramatic testimonies from street folk, prostitutes, or drugs addicts who have been raped, abused, tortured, and kidnapped. Of course the demons want to drag down, depress, and if possible, destroy as many unstable Christians as they can.

On the other hand, I think many Christians often exaggerate what the devil is doing. Many are quick to blame Satan, yet the works of the flesh, the lust of the flesh, and the pride of life are the primary reasons behind the fall of most Christians. Satan has not possessed them or taken over their life. Rather, they have chosen to enjoy the pleasures of sin instead of denying themselves and following disciplines and teachings of the Bible.

Restoration Is Not a Quick Fix

I appreciate sincere brothers and sisters laying hands on each other and praying for deliverance, but it takes a lot more than a few minutes of prayer. Restoration is not a quick fix, but a serious, long-term process. People who have engaged in deviant behavior or have developed life-dominating problems need time to be healed and restored to soundness of mind. The prayer of deliverance is not going to amount to anything without a strong commitment to follow up and rebuild the foundation and walls that have been broken down. Backsliders need to put off bad habits and put on new habits. They need to be retrained the right way the Bible way.

Why Reach Out?

The main reason for reaching out to backsliders is that God wants us to do it. God loves all His children and cares for them, no matter how badly they have gone astray or failed. The

Prodigal Son is the best example of that love. The Father was looking for him to come home and when he saw him from a faraway distance, he ran after him and displayed love and excitement.

He confirmed his love for his son. Unworthy, yet the son knew he was loved! Backsliders are insecure; they need to know we love them.

God's love for the backslider is our motivation. Yes, He hates sin, but He loves the sinner. As Christians, we have to constantly remind ourselves that we too are sinners. Our sins have been forgiven, but we still fall short of the glory. We must never forget that; if we do, we will quit reaching out to those in need. We will become gossipers instead of rescuers.

In Conclusion

I'm not proud of the failures in my life. I have been an extreme failure. I have hurt and disappointed hundreds of people. I can't change that reality. God has accepted and forgiven me. I can't take back what has happened in the past, but I can learn from my past and one day at a time live my future for the glory of God.

I have sinned severely against God and man! I can't blame my parents or other family members, I can't blame my bizarre childhood, I can't blame God for my failure. I can't blame Church leaders or Christians for my wretched sinful failures.

"I have sinned exceedingly in thought, word, and deed, by my fault, by my own fault, by my own most grievous fault. Especially, I accuse myself of the following sins..." From Saint Augustine's prayer book.

I want to thank the Church leaders and friends throughout the country who have been cheering me on and rejoicing with the angels in heaven over this one sinner who has come home.

Of course, without my wife, Sue, I doubt that I would have made it. She has been the strength in our marriage so many times. I know God gave her to me as a gift, and what a joy she has been! She has prayed, loved and cared for me. She took up her cross and denied herself. She did what was necessary to influence this backslider to surrender to the conviction of the Holy Spirit.

Most of all, I want to thank the Lord Jesus Christ for His everlasting love and amazing grace. To God be the glory!

O Lord, I ain't what I ought to be,
And I ain't what I want to be,
And I ain't what I'm going to be,
But O Lord, I thank you
That I ain't what I used to be!

(Author unknown)

A Word From Sue Premo:

It's been over seven years since Michael has had a drink or gone drugging on one of his sad, self-destructing journeys.

During the years of Michael's backsliding I could not even count how many times my heart was broken. There were many nights of crying out to the Lord on his behalf. I remember at one point I asked the Lord, "Why did you bring this man into my life?" I sensed the still, small voice of the Lord say to me, "To be his intercessor, Sue." I said, "God, was I not called to be his wife?" And again I sensed the still small voice of God say to me "... but I first called you to be his intercessor".

There were many times I was weary of praying for Mike but I knew that if I stopped, something horrible would happen.

I constantly battled depression. I never knew when Mike would take off to drink and drug. All I had to lean on was Jesus. I carried the shame and embarrassment of my backslidden husband.

Many Christians and even leaders counseled me to divorce my prodigal husband. I chose to forgive him and to love him back to Jesus.

I knew in my heart that my husband would someday return to the arms of the Lord, but I didn't have the insight as to how long it would take. I had to put it into the hands of God which wasn't easy.

In reflecting on some of the difficult times we've endured, I believe it has made our marriage and our love for God even stronger. Mike and I are best friends. I love him dearly.

Like Michael, I am a Christian in recovery. My healing continues.

We understand because we've been there. If we can help you or one of your loved ones, please don't hestitate to write or call.

Sincerely for backsliders,

Sue Premo

God loves legalistic, charismatic, sloppy agape, liberal, conservative, orthodox, southern, northern, black, white, denominational and nondenominational Christians.

God loves non-Christians. But, does God love backsliders? YES!!! ...for God is love!

Hosea 14:4 I will heal their backsliding, I will love them freely.

Jeremiah 3:14 Turn, O backsliding children, saith the Lord; for I am married to you:

> **In spite of all the sin and character flaws God says**
> *"I am married to you and I love you!"*

- Do you believe God loves you?
- Do you believe there is hope in your case?
- Are you a backslider?
- Do you want to stop backsliding?
- Do you want to really follow Jesus?

If you have answered YES to these questions please pray <u>now</u> and ask God to help you as you decide if you want to rededicate your life back to God. Your Heavenly Father wants you to come home! <u>The choice is yours.</u>

For confidential Christian counseling please call or write:

Christians In Recovery
PO BOX 98679
Des Moines, WA 98198-0679

(206) 870-7696

If you have made some kind of decision as a result of reading this book please consider writing us and letting us know what God is doing in your life.

The grace of the Lord Jesus Christ,
and the
love of God,
and the
communion of the Holy Spirit,
be with you all.
Amen.

Excerpts from some of the hundreds of letters this ministry has received.

Pray for me, I so often sicken of telling a lie to myself. However I still trust our Savior Jesus, I belong to Him and I can't find anything that will separate me from His love. *Mike, CA*

Currently I am in the Arizona State Prison serving a lengthy sentence. I'm here because I backslid badly into sin, and committed a crime. I have backslid many times and I've just about lost all hope. I'd like information about your ministry. *Jeff, AZ*

After my wife and I read your testimony we were so blessed and we could hardly believe what we read. In a two year period I left my wife and children four times. I was caught up in pornography and other sinful behavior. Maybe, as the Lord directs, we could start a chapter in this area. *Paul, OH*

Presently I'm incarcerated in a New Jersey County jail. I went to a Bible study class last night and the instructor gave me a magazine that featured an article on Mike Premo. I'm a 27 year old male, 6'5" 240 pound backslider. I'm believing God to mold and heal me. Please write me. Real soon! *Chester, NJ*

I'm trying to return to the Lord but have failed God so many times before. Please help me while I'm reaching out for the Lord! *Gary, WA*

I need spiritual counseling. I am Jewish and I love Jesus. I gave my life to Him when I was 12 but in my teens I backslid and got into drugs and boys. My husband is not a born again Christian, but I am praying for him. I want to grow in the Lord. My prayers and love are with you. *Marsha, WA*

Thanks for answering the phone when I called. Please don't quit praying for me. I feel at times I have been playing church. Could you send me information about your ministry. *Jeff, NY*

While reading Mike Premo's testimony I thought of my

six brothers who are all backslidden. Send information please. *Ann, Ontario*

I'm a backslidden Born-again, Spirit-filled Christian, and a recovering drug addict, alcoholic. *Susan, WA*

I have to be the biggest backslider ever. I've been in prison five years now. I've done some things that I believe are unforgivable. I've asked God into my life many times and yet sometimes I don't feel saved. I wish I could spend some time in your group. *AL, PA*

I'm serving a life sentence in this prison and I need to know the love of God. Will you include me in your prayers? I cannot count the number of times I have asked Christ into my life only to return to sin. *Herman, PA*

I'm a backslider who has lost my first love. My church broke up and I have family problems too serious and numerous to mention. It hurts and worries me because I want my faith restored. Regular Christians do not understand and all I get are the old clichés. *Muriel, Canada*

Mike Premo's story spoke to my heart and gave me hope and strength. I'm backsliding, drinking, sex, etc. I really need your prayers, please pray for me. I need the love of the Lord. *Victor, Alaska*

I'm presently serving a sentence of 37 years plus life at Folsom State Prison. After reading Mike Premo's testimony all I could think of was what a great God we have. I would like to know more about your ministry. I think it could have a great impact on the guys here.

Dear Brother Premo: I read your story today and it touched me and gave me hope that I need so desperately at this time in my life. I confess to you and mostly to God that I'm a backslider and I need help. As a child I was fascinated by pictures and magazines about sex. That grew into hard-core pornography, drugs, alcohol, prostitutes and so on. I would pray for forgiveness and it wouldn't be long before it would happen again. It seems my faith is at its lowest, I can't shake the guilt, the condemnation. It seems like God has abandoned me. I need Him, I need His love. People in church think I'm fine. I haven't told anybody about these things but my wife, you and God. I am a deacon in my church. I wish I could talk to you face-to-face. I need your prayers. What should I do? God bless you and your wife. *Ronnie, NC*

I am a backslider and trying hard to find my way back to the Lord Jesus Christ. I have been a homosexual. Thanks for your concern. *Walt, GA*

I am a former minister. I am presently incarcerated with a ten year sentence for incest. I have a great deal of remorse and self-condemnation. Could you send me information about your ministry and anything that could help concerning my area of sin. Please respond soon. *Fred, MD*

I am interested in starting a chapter in Las Vegas. I am a recovered alcoholic and compulsive gambler with a few years behind me. *Ingrid, NV*

> Thus saith the Lord,
> *"Return, ye backsliding children,
> and I will heal your backslidings."*
> Jeremiah 3:22

**If you want to backslide
that's your business**

**If you want to stop
that's our business**

This ministry is available day or night to offer counseling or prayer to anyone feeling the need. For a free copy of our newsletter or further information about our work, please write or call.

Christians in Recovery
PO Box 98679
Des Moines, WA 98198-0769
(206) 870-7696

"Hurting people getting help—By helping hurting people"

How To Stop Backsliding

By Michael Premo

... If you do these things, you will never fall:

2 Peter 1:10

How To Stop Backsliding the follow-up book to *Backslider* is now available. The total cost including postage and handling is $7.00.

An audio cassette of Michael Premo's testimony is available for $6.00.

Michael Premo is available for speaking engagements by contacting the office of *Christians In Recovery*.